CHINESE
STONEWARE
GLAZES

CHINESE STONEWARE GLAZES

BY JOSEPH GREBANIER

Photography of the author's work by Paul E. Grebanier

WATSON-GUPTILL PUBLICATIONS/NEW YORK

PITMAN PUBLISHING/LONDON

Copyright © 1975 by Joseph Grebanier

First published 1975 in the United States and Canada by Watson-Guptill Publications,
a division of Billboard Publications, Inc.,
One Astor Plaza, New York, N.Y. 10036

Library of Congress Cataloging in Publication Data
Grebanier, Joseph, 1912–
  Chinese stoneware glazes.
  Bibliography: p.
  Includes index.
  1. Glazing (Ceramics) 2. Pottery, Chinese.
3. Glazes. I. Title.
TT922.G73 1975   738.1'44   74-23115
ISBN 0-8230-0625-5

Published in Great Britain by Sir Isaac Pitman & Sons Ltd.,
39 Parker Street, London WC2B 5PB
ISBN 0-273-00909-5

Manufactured in U.S.A.

First Printing, 1975

Edited by Sarah Bodine
Designed by Bob Fillie
Set in 11 point Baskerville by Harold Black, Inc.

For Lillian
. . . *sine qua, nihil*

CONTENTS

1. THE SECRET OF LIGHT BLUE CHÜN, 15

2. KUAN-CHÜN:
A BRIDGE BETWEEN CHÜN AND CELADON, 23

3. OTHER VARIETIES OF CELADON, 29

4. DARK BLUE-AND-BROWN MOTTLED GLAZES, 65

5. COPPER RED AND PEACH BLOOM, 69

6. TURQUOISE, 79

7. TEMMOKU, 83

8. TZ'U-CHOU, 93

9. GLAZES IN COMBINATION, 97

10. ADVENTURES WITH OLD AND NEW GLAZES, 101

11. STONEWARE BODIES,
SLIPS, STAINS, AND UNDERGLAZE, 111

12. GLAZE CALCULATION, 115

13. SYNTHETIC WOOD ASH, 127

APPENDIX, 132

ACKNOWLEDGMENTS

This book offers a detailed account of the procedures I have developed over a period of many years in the making of stoneware glazes belonging to several different families of Chinese ceramics, especially those of the Sung era. My observations and methods have probably been neither more nor less original than, say, those of the Koryo potters who were attempting an approximation of either the fabled Ju ware or the so-called Northern Celadon. As in the Korean case, the outcomes have, I think, justified the effort. In varying degrees, some of the glazes I have evolved, particularly the light blue Chün, the Kuan and the Lung-ch'üan variety of celadons, as well as the Ch'ing copper reds, are apparently authentic evocations of the past; others, though truly blood relatives, are, to my knowledge, without identical antecedents anywhere. All have given me pleasure, both in the seeking and in the finding. More important, I am certain that other potters can build to good advantage on what I have done. Hence this book.

But before passing on to my own findings, acknowledgment must be made of the many influences without which these pages would never have been written. Foremost among them is the fine artist and my valued friend, David Holleman, who first guided me into an appreciation and an understanding of good, honest potting. From my association with him I gained a host of invaluable things: the standards for and the practical technique of making a satisfactory pot, a deepened insight into the theory of glaze calculation, a great variety of glazes of his own composition, both earthenware and stoneware, the basic elements of firing procedure, experience in kiln construction, and, above all, an aesthetic rapport with the best in stoneware. In short, he started me on the road that ultimately brought me to my own Chün, Kuan, and temmoku glazes, to name just a few. I am certain that no such results would have been obtained without his early encouragement, advice, and criticism.

I also owe special thanks to Dr. Walter D. Kring, whose whole-hearted enthusiasm in the cause of fine ceramics and whose kind offers to rake up the cudgels on behalf of this book have greatly encouraged me in making it available to the public. In addition, his close reading of the original manuscript resulted in some very useful criticisms and suggestions.

Similarly, I am indebted to editors Don Holden, Diane Hines, and Sarah Bodine for their invaluable advice on format, as well as for the impetus their questions and suggestions gave to my rethinking many ideas so much more productively.

All the other influences I feel deeply indebted to have been (with the notable exception of one) the occasional, seminal ones of the printed page. Here the most inspiring book has been that almost sibylline little volume by A. L. Hetherington, *Chinese Ceramic Glazes*. Again and again, I have returned to its pages for an illuminating paragraph here, a suggestive phrase there, despite the fact that it contains not a single glaze recipe. Of general technical assistance, too, and a source of almost adventitious inspiration has been C. W. Parmelee's massive compilation, *Ceramic Glazes*. And, of course, simply in terms of inspired standards rather than specific techniques, Bernard Leach's *A Potter's Book* has been truly valuable.

For the rest, I have gained very important technical stimulation from such publications as the *Transactions of the British Ceramic Society*, in the pages of which first appeared Moore and Mellor's trail-blazing articles on copper reds. Of even more direct aid in my work on this particular group of glazes was the study by T. Yoshioka and S. Hiroaka as reported in the *Abstracts* of the same Society. In addition, certain very important points about the firing of these same glazes were first brought to my attention in the work of C. M. Harder. To another Japanese researcher, Tsuneshi Ishii, in his account of his experiments with Kinuta blue celadon glazes, I am indebted for one of the colorant approaches I occasionally have used in some of my celadons. Other than in the few sources I have thus far specified, or shall mention later, the reader will probably come across no other repetitions elsewhere in print of the ceramic compositions I shall detail in these pages.

Finally, special tribute must be paid to the one other human being whose personal influence has been indispensable to me: my wife Lillian. Her keen aesthetic enjoyment of all that is best in ceramic art, her unflagging encouragement, even her willingness to become, on occasion, a kind of "pottery widow," no less than her fearless and constructive criticism, all have confirmed for me the value of the quest itself and have helped determine its direction.

INTRODUCTION

This, of course, is a book exclusively on glazes. But it would be somewhat precipitate to launch into the subject without first admitting, at least in passing, that good form rather than good glaze is the basis of good pottery. No glaze, no matter how beautifully composed, applied, and fired, can do more than partly compensate for poorly conceived or clumsily executed form.

Yet it is a serious error to infer from this fact the converse idea that glaze is merely decorative, merely a kind of garment that superficially covers what is beneath and, in a sense, is detached from it. A stoneware glaze of the best kind not only has a character and an appeal of its own, but it is *integral* with the pot; it blends in and forms an intimate harmony with the body it envelops. Thus, form and glaze become inseparable parts of an aesthetic whole. It is therefore no accident that the history of connoisseurship in Far Eastern ceramics is chiefly oriented to glaze as such, although linked with particular shapes and styles of potting. Most of the emphasis in the terminology and the identification of the different kinds of ware, especially Chinese stonewares of the Sung period, has been placed on the characteristics of the glazes. The major part of the attributions made by authorities in this area is based on such considerations as the color, texture, depth, and density of glaze, first and foremost, with certain aspects of body and form usually adduced as supportive evidence.

I stress this apparent preeminence of glaze for a variety of reasons. First, I believe it is the beauty of Oriental glazes that has been especially responsible for the elevation of pottery to the rank of a major art. That ceramics can be, and indeed is, a major art, at least in the classic work that has come from China, Japan, and Persia, is attested by the importance given to it in collection after collection treasured in the great art museums all over the world. And, of course, there is the simple fact of the great monetary value placed, especially in the Orient, on individual pieces of ceramic art; a value, incidentally, that equates in sheer dollars and cents with some of the fantastic sums spent on both modern and classic oil paintings in the West. I grant that these facts may well be taken as rather superficial proof. But at their root is an aesthetic reality; namely, the large measure of delight and wonder that a ceramic masterpiece can arouse in the beholder. And this aesthetic reality would doubtless vanish if all the classic glazes of the Orient were miraculously to be stripped from the ware. It may be that another, entirely different aesthetic would remain, based on the color, texture, and pure form of the fired clay, and these can be lovely things, but it would offer a much diminished experience.

I therefore see a great inconsistency between the general acclaim bestowed on the wonderful glazes of the classic past and the dearth of beautiful glazes being made in our time. One of the common clichés among art potters of this part of the twentieth century is the statement that only "one or two" glazes are needed, or indeed should be used, in one's work. Instead, stylish experiments with form, surface texture, and decoration are preferred, even if they are endlessly repetitious of each other. Anything else is considered "derivative" (a most pejorative label) and not truly creative. Quite deliberately, however, some few of us have followed our own bent, regardless of momentary fashions, and have drawn fresh inspiration from those same works of the past that speak most directly to us. In the case of the glazes described in these pages, they happen to be most often, though not exclusively, the ceramic masterpieces of the Sung era in China. There is really no reason to set an uncrossable gap between connoisseurship and creation; otherwise, one would be forced, in the interests of mere logic, to condemn an artist like Modigliani, for example, because he failed to separate his love of African sculpture from his own work. In any case, no sincere artist can be expected to make images to gods he does *not* worship, no matter how fashionable they may be.

Sung pottery being unthinkable without Sung glazes, it was natural and inevitable, therefore, that one with my particular bent should do careful research and make many hundreds of experiments in the direction of these glazes. The result, most happily, has been a certain number of more or less authentic Oriental glazes newly constituted, others that are equally attractive variants of these, plus some that have never been created before.

At the same time, there has been impressed on me a rather inescapable, technical conclusion; namely, that a great many of the apparently different Sung glazes were really variants of *one* basic approach to glaze formulation and production. More specifically, the whole varied family of glazes known as celadons — Yüeh, Lung-ch'üan, Kuan, Ko, Ju, Ch'ing-pai, and Northern Celadon, plus the Koryo of Korea and that special Chinese Sung type known as Chün — all of these are actually much closer to each other in composition than the somewhat shadowy, separating classifications of connoisseurs would seem to suggest. Practically all these glazes are essentially similar because almost all contain in varying degrees, it seems to me, not only a high proportion of feldspar, a good deal of flint, and a small amount of clay, generously fluxed by such agents as limestone, but also — and this is the significant point — a certain amount of *wood ash*. I know that more than one authority has indicated wood ash as an interesting component of an occasional glaze or so. But I see it, rather, as the almost omnipresent contributor to a whole range of supposedly different glazes.

Even as late as the K'ang Hsi period, in the Ch'ing dynasty, ash from a mixture of bracken fern and limestone calcined together in alternating layers was reported by the Jesuit missionary, Père d'Entrecolles. Describing the process in his long letter from China in 1712, he refers to the no-longer-available *wood* ash "from the tree *Se-tse*," and adds: "It was perhaps owing to this wood that the porcelain made in early times is more beautiful than that which is made nowadays." He also notes that even the bracken ash, which I would consider (from his description of the process of prepara-tion) to bulk very small in volume as compared to the lime, varies in "esteem" as to its source, from place to place.

Equally relevant here as to the universality of wood ash in Far Eastern glaze compositions is the fairly recent discovery (reported in Gompertz's book on Koryo celadons) of glaze test fragments at a Korean kiln site of the late 13th century. These fragments "were inscribed in iron pigment along the edge with characters which are thought to give the formula of the glaze." Some of these characters apparently denote "such ingredients as red clay and wood ash."

I must also add, since it is of equal importance, that included in this basic mixture of feldspar, flint, clay, limestone, and wood ash is a small but significant proportion of *iron*. Without iron, no Sung glaze of any type — celadon, Chün, temmoku, and even Ting — could have been created. With the various celadons, of course, it helps produce colors that range all the way from olive green to light green, gray, delicate blue-green, and blue itself. The clay slips basic to the dark brown and black temmokus are heavily charged with iron. The distinctively white Ting ware runs from cream color to blue-white, depending on the relative degree of oxidation or reduction of the tiny amount of iron present. And the vivianite blue of Chün is clearly owing to the union of phosphorus and iron.

The probable genesis of these glazes is intriguing. It is self-evident that before the discovery of glaze, pots were fired without any other surface treatment than incising, impressing, clay-painted decorations, and so on. Since the original fuel for the firings most naturally was wood, it was inevitable that, in the course of time and quite by accident, a by-product of the firing process, the wood ash itself, should become sig-nificantly involved with both the flames and the ware inside the kiln. This involvement of the ash with the ware must have first become noticeable as higher temperatures were reached. The evidence is clear on numerous *un*glazed stoneware pots preserved from early times; in some cases, these pots have a brownish green gloss either on one side or on their shoulders and lips. We also have, probably from a somewhat later date, stone-ware pots that have this same speckled brownish green glaze as a thin overall covering. The explanation is simple: in the first instance, because of the natural draught created by the flames in the fire grates, flecks of wood ash were drawn into the kiln and were caught by the nearest pots, either on one side (the side nearer the flames) or on protruding shoulders and lips (on which the ash could most easily settle), and combin-ing with the clay of the pots' surfaces, thus became a thin, brownish glaze. The next important step, inspired by the Chinese potter's observation, was the deliberate sprin-kling of wood ash all over a newly made pot while it was still moist and then firing the two together when dry.

At this moment, what was ultimately to become the glory of Chinese Sung pottery was born. For from this same moment on, the early Chinese potter must have gradually begun to realize that he had limitless supplies of a valuable fluxing agent for the creation of hard, impermeable glazes, glazes that seemed to be in "stone-like" harmony with the high-fired pottery they covered. With the forests of wood he regularly burned as fuel for his kiln, he could make huge quantities of this ideal stoneware glaze com-ponent. The bodies of the pots he worked with were luckily formed of rather refractory clays and so could stand up to the high temperatures needed for the maturing of stoneware glazes. The only unexplained part of this remarkable development in technique is the advent of feldspar as such into the total picture. Conjecturally, attempts at the use of only partly decomposed feldspar as "clay" for bodies or slips may have induced experiment, especially when this material was observed as interacting with the wood ash sprinklings. (As reported in Laufer's *The Beginnings of Porcelain in China*, the analysis by H. W. Nichols of the chemical composition of several Han proto-porcelain pieces, apparently bearing the earliest Chinese feldspathic glazes ever identified as such, points in the same direction. Nichols felt that the body and the glaze contained such similar materials that the glaze may have been "prepared by mixing the material of the body with pulverized limestone." He later adds: "It is of course possible that the potters had learned to adjust the qualities of the glaze by small additions of alkali and iron oxide.") Or perhaps the inclusion of feldspar slabs or veins among the rocks that helped form the interior masonry of the earliest stoneware kilns, reacting in the same way, may have inspired creative observation along the same lines. Of course, without archaeological remains (like the ash-glazed pots which we do have) to test the validity of the latter surmise, it remains just that.

At this point, certain reservations must be made about my arguments for the relative omnipresence of wood ash in Sung glazes. The whole idea sounds dangerously like a thesis; and, like so many others, it is for that very reason somewhat suspect. To some degree, then, the idea needs modification in keeping with demonstrable facts. One such fact is that later on, by Ch'ing times, despite some limited use of fern ash, phosphorus had practically disappeared as an element of Chinese glazes. The result is observable in the essentially glassy, more unobstructedly transparent quality of the clear Ch'ing glazes, especially the celadons. In the typical Sung glaze, instead, the presence of phosphorus via wood ash adds a myriad of bubbles to a glaze's structure and thereby tends to increase both its relative opacity and its apparent depth; it also has a distinct effect on color, especially in the case of blue-green celadons and Chün. Another fact that must curtail the scope of my idea about wood ash is the simple one that a few of my own best celadons, for example, contain no wood ash and hence little or no phosphorus. Of course, in keeping with the noted characteristics of Ch'ing glazes, these particular celadons of mine also tend to be clearer, glassy transparents, though a few have greater depth and a noticeable diffusion of bubbles throughout. Phosphorus is not the sole cause of bubbling.

These reservations leave me with another conclusion: it is unreasonable to expect diverse individual potters and potteries to be uniform in technique. On the contrary, it is hard not to assume that some Sung and Yüan potters would be tempted to try varying their existing glaze formulations with the *omission* of wood ash. Thus the way was probably paved for much of the Ming and most Ch'ing glazes. The increased slickness of the result in some cases would have had an immediate appeal to some; and eventually a "trend" would have been established. I obviously question the value of the gains as compared to the losses.

Thus far I have confined my remarks on glaze technique to the question of basic *composition*. Before concluding, it remains to make some general observations about the *firing process*, as this is equally important in determining the character of the glaze. (This all important matter will be gone into in terms of actual procedures in Chapter 1, as well as later.) Temperature I have already mentioned; for most Sung-type glazes it should normally be no less than 2300°F. (1260°C.). But the distinctive quality of each glaze depends to a great extent on the *atmosphere* inside the kiln. In a kiln firing, there are essentially *two* possible atmospheres: one that *oxidizes* and one that *reduces*. The difference can be symbolized by the difference between a clear, bright flame and a smoldering, smoky one.

In the presence of a sufficiency of oxygen, or an oxidizing atmosphere, a metal like iron will usually cause a glaze to turn such colors as brown, tan, yellow, brownish black, or brownish red. Copper, on the other hand, will produce greens and blues under oxidation.

The process of reduction is quite different in its effects. By depriving the kiln atmosphere of the oxygen normally added to it by air, reduction forces the glaze components to turn inward on themselves, so to speak, and to the clay body beneath them, in order to obtain the oxygen needed for combustion. The process thus forces a *reduction in the oxygen content* of such glaze colorants as iron oxide and copper oxide and turns them more or less into *metallic* iron and copper. So it is that reduced iron helps turn glazes green, black, or, perhaps most interesting, blue. Reduced copper, on the other hand, yields shades ranging from deep red to delicate pink. It should be stressed that the greens and blues of oxidized copper are quite different from those gained from reduced iron; equally different are the reds created separately by oxidized iron and reduced copper.

Now we are ready to turn to specific glazes and techniques.

1
THE SECRET OF LIGHT BLUE CHÜN

It is wise to begin with a glaze that offers the fullest opportunity to describe the entire range of activities and materials that go into its creation. Such a glaze is light blue Chün, one of the loveliest at its best, often ranging from a soft but vibrant periwinkle blue to subtler effects that are tinged with green or flecked with tan or brown. The texture is a soft, thick semi-matte, verging in some cases into a brilliant translucency.

In this basic chapter, I shall explain every process necessary to this one glaze, from beginning to end, so that *all* the essential information is in one practical sequence (rather than thinly scattered among separate chapters, each on a different aspect of glaze making). For the succeeding glazes, I shall refer the reader back to the procedures explained here, taking care to note any significant differences of procedure, material, or result.

Like many of the other glazes I shall describe, the Chün requires a certain amount of wood ash in its formulation. So I shall start with an account of the preparation of this one material.

Wood Ash

The best ash for the Chün effect is made from softwoods like white pine and spruce. I have obtained the raw materials for this substance from two sources: either my own fireplace in New Hampshire or the waste fires of small lumber companies that use white pine almost exclusively.

Preparing Wood Ash

The first step, after obtaining these ashes, is the process of washing them. A large receptacle, such as an old wash tub, is ideal for the purpose. The ashes are first picked over a bit by hand to remove any especially large lumps of charcoal, partly burned wood, or nails and glass. Then generous quantities of water are added until several inches of it are standing above the ashes when they have settled. Then the ashes and water are stirred together vigorously with a large stick so that the floating pieces of remaining charcoal and wood can be sieved off and thrown away. After more very thorough stirring, the ashes-and-water should be allowed to stand for three or four hours.

When the ashes have plainly settled out several inches below the water level, as much of the liquid which can be poured or siphoned off without disturbing the ashes should be removed and discarded. (This liquid is undesirable for our special purposes because it is rich in soluble, alkaline substances that would later tend to make the glaze itself quite unstable in its application to the ware.) The ash is then thoroughly stirred and more fresh water is added and mixed with it. Over a period of about three days, the processes of removing the alkaline liquids and then stirring in fresh water are repeated some seven or eight times. The final pour-off should consist of water that is relatively clear and tasteless.

At this point, we are ready to dry the ashes. This can be done in several ways or by a combination of them: the ashes can be ladled out in lumps into separate pans or onto a set of broad, flat forms and exposed to warm sunlight; they can be dried in pots and pans over stoves; or they can be dried on plaster bats reserved solely for this purpose. Finally, the fully dried lumps of ash can be crumbled by hand, sifted through a 50- or 60-mesh screen, and stored in strong paper bags or in glass containers. We now have ready for use a material of only generally defined chemical composition. (This fact negates any useful attempt at a reliable empirical ceramic formula. However, in Chapter 13, analyses and formulas for *synthetic* wood ash are presented that have proved serviceable.) But, judging from the resulting glaze, the ash is quite rich in potash, sodium, phosphorus, and silicates, as well as iron. In any case, it is essential to my Chün glaze.

Chün Glaze Recipe: CIH-p

The best batch recipe I have arrived at for a light blue Chün glaze follows:

Buckingham feldspar	56.
Flint	22.
Whiting	13.
Softwood ash	9.
	100.
Yellow ochre (2.5% of batch)	2.5

The proportion of ash used (9%) may seem small; but I have found through careful experimentation that much larger proportions merely have a dulling effect on the glaze by excessively increasing its opacity. In fact, the desired blue effect completely disappears.

Mixing the Glaze Ingredients

Once the glaze batch has been weighed out, the process of mixing it presents at least a couple of possibilities, depending on subtle differences in the resulting glazes desired by the potter. For an interesting, more mottled effect, the glaze ingredients may be dry-milled *without* water in a ball mill for about one hour, or the simpler but more laborious method of dry-sifting through a 50-mesh screen may be substituted for small test quantities of glaze. The dry glaze can then be stored in glass jars until needed.

For a more even effect of unvariegated blue, I usually *wet*-mill the glaze ingredients with just enough water to produce a mix of about the consistency of light cream. After about one hour of wet-milling, the glaze is strained off through a wide-meshed kitchen sieve into a basin; to this I also add the light rinsings (with four or five ounces of fresh water) from the ball mill and its pebbles. I then pour the glaze mix into glass jars where it is allowed to settle for a few days. Later, I siphon off and discard the extra water on the surface in each jar to bring the consistency of the glaze down to that of heavy cream. An ordinary rubber bulb-syringe, such as is often used to add water to car batteries, makes the most manageable siphon in this case.

Applying the Glaze

Once the glaze is mixed with water to the consistency of heavy cream it is ready for application to the ware. (Dry-milled glazes, of course, will also require the careful addition of just the right amount of water to achieve this same consistency.) In my experience, I have consistently applied my glazes to ware previously bisqued at no more than Orton cone 06 (approximately 1832°F. or 1000°C.), and have used an air-pressure spray gun for the glazing of all surfaces except for the inner surfaces of bottles, teapots, narrow vases, and the like.

1. Glazing the Interiors of Narrow-Mouthed Containers. For the inner surfaces of these, I thin out a moderate quantity of the glaze mixture with a small amount of additional water until the glaze is quite fluid and no longer creamy. This thinned mixture is poured into the bottle or other narrow-shaped ware, sometimes with the aid of a funnel, swished around evenly inside by rotating the pot itself at a slight tilt in the hands, and then gradually poured back out of it while still in rotation. Thus all the inner surfaces are coated with glaze; its thickness depends both on how long the glaze is allowed to remain inside and on how much water has been used to thin the glaze. In any case, this method of pouring thinned glaze into such wares does add a certain amount of unwanted moisture to the body of a pot; so it is advisable, before spraying the outer surfaces of such pieces, to set them aside to dry for several hours, or better yet overnight.

2. Adding Gum to the Glaze. Before spraying, I usually add about two teaspoons of corn syrup (such as Karo) to roughly a pint of glaze to keep it from dusting off excessively on my fingers during later handling of the sprayed pots. Such dusting off can create ugly bare or thinned spots in the fired glaze.

3. Spraying Glaze on the Bottom of the Pot. Using the sprayer at relatively low pressure, I first apply the glaze to the lower and outer surfaces of, say, an open bowl as I spin it around on a hand-operated banding wheel. For this purpose, I invert the pot on a removable bat (made of thin wallboard), cover its foot with a circular piece of linoleum of about the same size as the foot, and slowly rotate the wheel while spraying from about 8″ away.

For narrow-mouthed containers, of course, this step is actually the second one, since their inner surfaces will already have been coated with glaze by pouring, as explained above. In any case, bottles, jars, or vases with even slightly rounded lower contours should also be inverted for the initial part of exterior glazing. These rounded, lower contours should be sprayed before the upper areas. A pre-fired clay chuck is a very useful device for holding such forms, particularly bottles, in the inverted position.

Note: It is important to avoid overwetting the pot with the glaze; otherwise, the glaze will peel in patches from the pot during the firing and will later come from the kiln disfigured by large crawl marks. Therefore, one should be careful (1) not to have too much water in the glaze mix, and (2) not to continue spraying when the surface of the pot begins to get a shiny or soaked, "wet-through" look.

4. Cleaning the Foot. After the outer surface of the ware has been sprayed, its foot should be wiped clean on the edges with a *dry* sponge, and the ware replaced on the banding wheel right side up, preferably on a clean bat surface free of glaze.

5. Spraying the Top of the Pot. The spraying should be finished by evenly coating the inside of the pot and its rim while the wheel is rotating. The same caution about overwetting should be observed.

For narrow-mouthed containers (already glazed inside), this step will be required for the upper, *exterior* portions, instead. At the same time, the upper and lower coatings should be carefully and evenly graded into each other so as to leave no mark or line of separation between the two.

Drying the Glaze

The next step is drying the glaze. It must be stressed that any hurrying of this process, especially at the beginning, will result in the same kind of ugly peeling and crawling caused by overwetting. Ideally, the sprayed ware should be allowed to dry for about one week in a relatively airy but quiet area of moderate temperature. Once the exposed, unglazed foot of the pot feels dry and no cooler to the touch than the prevailing room temperature, the pot is ready for stacking and firing.

The Kiln

Of course, the type of kiln used is one of the most variable factors in the whole process. A brief description of the kiln I have used for firing the glazes detailed in this book might be helpful. It is an updraft, natural gas-fired kiln very similar to the test kilns of the Alpine Company of El Segundo, California. There are two fireholes admitting flames into a baffled channel on either side of a half-muffled stacking area, the latter being about 23″ high, 16″ deep, and 16″ wide. Air is mixed with the gas at controlled ratios by means of a small blower, and is quantitatively keyed to both the gas and the amount of flue opening variously arranged during the firing. The flue opening is adjusted by moving two K-bricks (insulating bricks, in the U.K. called H.T.I. bricks) at the top of the short center chimney. Two bricked-in flue-ways above the arch lead to this chimney from either side of the kiln interior.

Stacking the Kiln. For the Chün effect, a pot must be fired in a reduction firing schedule. It is therefore pertinent to stress here that ideally the kiln should be closely packed with pots. Also, assuming that the potter is intimately aware of the idiosyncrasies of his kiln (gas fired, it is to be hoped), it is essential that he select an area in the kiln where reduction will be heaviest and the temperature highest, if he is to achieve the full beauties of the blue Chün glaze. In my kiln, and in many others, both the heaviest reduction and the highest work-heat usually occur in the middle levels of the kiln. The two extremes at top and bottom of the kiln are the least dependable for these purposes. Even the quite sophisticated eighteenth-century Chinese kilns observed by Père d'Entrecolles illustrated this same peculiarity (see *Bibliography*); both these extremes were habitually stacked with *empty* saggers, because any ware placed in them would have been "insufficiently fired." In the case of Chün in my kiln, then, the authentic blue color can be achieved to the fullest degree most consistently if the stacking is done in the *middle* levels.

It is my own practice to pre-stack the kiln with the bisqued ware *before* it is glazed as a sort of "dry run" to plan just which pieces will go where and which glazes will be used on which pieces. I then make a shelf-by-shelf record of both these sets of facts, which later serves me in several ways: (1) it facilitates glazing the pieces just as I had intended; (2) it is a sure guide to re-stacking the *glazed* pieces in the kiln for the actual firing with a minimum of handling; and (3) it is a permanent record of successes and failures in terms of glaze placement in the kiln for a particular pattern of firing.

Firing the Kiln for Heavy Reduction. Since our Chün-glazed pot is to be fired to a full Orton cone 10 work-heat, a pat of cones 8, 9, and 10 must be placed within view of the front peephole during the stacking of the kiln. A portable kiln pyrometer is also needed during the firing for readings to be taken at the front peephole.

Incidentally, the pat holding the pyrometric cones can most easily be made from a small amount of coarse sagger-clay mix, consisting of ball clay (50%), China biscuit grog (25%), and flint (25%). Once the cones have been placed in it at the usual slight angle, and the whole pat smoothed and firmed around them, top and bottom, I usually pierce the pat full of tiny holes on all sides with a blunted needle. Such a rugged but "well-ventilated" cone pat dries quickly, is in no danger of exploding during the firing, and is completely refractory, both at cone 10 and well above.

The following firing procedure is given in terms of the kiln described above; another kiln will require somewhat different adjustments to obtain similar conditions.

1. First, there is a warming-up period of one hour during which only the pilot lights are on, the gas being mixed with a slight amount of air from the blower. All three peepholes are left open, and the two flue bricks are wide apart with the fullest aperture (about 5″ square) between them. To keep the pilots from being blown out by the force of the blower air, I have found it helpful to set long slender sticks of K-brick into the fire ports just an inch or two in front of each pilot.

2. Next, the main burners are turned on, and the regular firing begins with the "water-smoking" period. The first section of this phase is completed in the next one-and-a-quarter hours, at the end of which time the three peepholes are closed with round K-brick plugs. The flues at the stack, it should be noted, still remain wide open. During this short period, both gas and air are gradually increased from moderate beginnings to a flame that is approximately three-quarters the intensity of the flame utilized in the latter part of the firing.

3. These conditions prevail unchanged for about another hour and a half, until a pyrometric reading taken at the front peephole shows the kiln temperature to be about 1450°F. (786°C.).

4. At this point, the flue opening is narrowed to an aperture of about 3¼″ and the volume of gas sufficiently increased to produce a moderate degree of reduction within the kiln. This condition can be checked by the appearance, just above the chimney and under the chimney hood, of a slight amount of light blue flame. This is especially true when using natural gas, propane, or oil. Another check is the presence of some back pressure at the front peephole.

5. The conditions indicated in Step 4 should be maintained for about a half hour, after which the volume of gas should again be increased to what will probably be the point of fullest intensity. (*Note:* This does *not* mean using the full volume of gas available in the supply pipes, which may well be about 2″ in diameter! Only a modest proportion of what is available should ever be used.) The additional gas and a slightly more narrowed flue opening of about 3″ will naturally mean even more reduction: the blue flame at the stack will be heavier and the back pressure at the peephole will be greater.

6. The previous period should terminate when a pyrometer inserted at the front peephole gives a reading of 1850°F. (1010°C.). At this point, the fullest reduction is to be contrived as follows: The bricks atop the chimney are pushed close together, leaving as little opening as possible between them. At the same time, the air blower, though still operating, should have its air intake almost completely closed off. In addition, the volume of gas should be *decreased* to the point where the long yellow flame from each burner reaches about two-thirds into the kiln. (In my kiln, I can check this fact visually via the two primary air holes, level with the floor channels, on either side of the kiln.)

The appearance of the reducing kiln during this period, which should last three-quarters of an hour, may be somewhat frightening at first, with flames licking and leaping out of all available cracks and openings, and black clouds of carbon dioxide pouring up into the hood and spouting out together with yellow flame from any of the three peepholes that may be temporarily opened. But with adequate kiln room ventilation and careful supervision by the potter, there is nothing to fear. In my opinion, and judging from my own experience, there is really no other way of achieving an authentically blue Chün effect. I have tried the more genteel approaches to reduction firing recommended by some authorities; though they may be adequate for certain effects, they are not really adequate for most of my reduction glazes, at least not in my kiln.

7. After the three-quarters-of-an-hour period of heaviest reduction described in step 6 is over, the flue opening is again returned to about 3″, and the gas volume is increased to fullest firing intensity (that is, to what it had been prior to the full reduction phase). At the same time, the air blower intake is opened to permit a somewhat greater admixture of air than was utilized before the early stages of the heavy reduction periods. Again, the stack will exhibit a fairly heavy thick blue flame, and the peepholes a somewhat smoky back pressure.

8. This step encompasses a few stages of approximately one-half to three-quarters of an hour each, during which air, gas, and flue openings are adjusted to produce a gradual change at the stack towards a *lighter* volume of blue flame. At the last of these stages, the blue flame should still be fully discernible; otherwise, there is a danger of oxidation taking over inside the kiln.

The adjustments may then be left as they are until shut-off time, although periodic checking on the progress of the firing is advisable. One very important thing to check is the light blue flame at the stack: it must never be permitted to disappear altogether, for much of the benefit of the earlier reduction would vanish with it.

9. Finally, after about nine hours or so from the start of firing, the first pyrometric cone in the pat of three (8, 9, and 10) will begin to bend. When, almost an hour later, cone 10 is well bent over and resting on the already deformed cones 9 and 8, the firing should be stopped. (Dark sunglasses make it easier for the potter to view the cones through the peephole in the dazzling glare of the kiln's interior.) I then shut off simultaneously the air blower and the gas, shove the flue bricks tight together, and stop up or cover over with pieces of K-brick every opening on the outside of the kiln.

10. The "cracking" or opening of the kiln should be a gradual affair, and should not start until at least twelve hours later, when the first bits of K-brick are removed from the odd openings (like the side primary holes). A few hours later, I can safely remove the peephole plugs; I follow this somewhat later with separating the two flue bricks about an inch from each other; still later, several inches; and so on.

11. Then, with drafts and ventilation in the kiln room kept to a minimum, the kiln door itself can be opened bit by bit. At last, the pots, still hot to the hand (assuming the potter is of the usual impatient type!), are removed from the kiln with the aid of asbestos gloves. Greater patience is of course advisable to prevent possible dunting or freakish craze lines, but it is a very rare human quality.

The Finished Pot

The resulting Chün-glazed pot may vary considerably in texture, color, and mottling, depending on the body used (whether buff or red), placement in the kiln, degree of reduction, and the methods and materials used in preparing and applying the glaze itself. Those specimens that most closely resemble the true Chün glaze of Sung times are an unctuous semi-matte with a soft, light, but warm blue of great depth owing, in part, to the mass of tiny bubbles entrapped in the glaze itself. Both the color and the cloudy, rich texture of the glaze are induced by the presence of phosphorus (from the wood ash) and by the process of reduction. Equally important for the blue color is the presence of iron, introduced by means of the yellow ochre, which combines with the phosphorus to form ferrous phosphate, or the often vividly blue mineral, vivianite.

Examination of the clay body of the pot, either at the unglazed foot or in cross-section (when broken), will reveal a heavily reduced coloration. Depending on the body composition, this coloration will vary from a light gray to a dark, chocolate brown. It is never the buff or bright red colors of oxidized clay.

A Chün Glaze Variant: CIHp-F2

A somewhat darker effect of great visual and tactile appeal can be gained by substituting other forms of iron for the yellow ochre in the glaze batch recipe. For example, I have used black iron oxide (2.5% also) for that purpose. On a buff body (one that therefore reduces to gray or brown), the resulting glaze (CIHp-F2), especially when wet-milled one hour in preparation, fires to a texture and a color somewhat resembling those of Kuan ware, though bluer; on a red stoneware body, the blue ranges from dense clouds of very soft light blue to darker passages going off into brown.

2
KUAN-CHÜN:
A BRIDGE BETWEEN
CHÜN AND CELADON

Celadon glazes are the very heart of fine Chinese ceramics, particularly those of the Sung dynasty. Their closeness in color and texture to jade, aesthetically valued by the ancient Chinese above all other gems, is one basic explanation of this fact. And like jade, celadons represent a large and varied range of types answering to a number of different, traditional names: Kuan, Lung-ch'üan, Ko, Ju, Northern Celadon, and the derivative Korean Koryo, to cite just the principal ones. For each of these types, I have developed glazes that more or less mirror the beauty of the originals. But the question of exact type designation is admittedly one that becomes rather subjective, the more one looks into it.

The Problem of Attribution

If one reads at all extensively in this field, and studies the celadon specimens themselves, one is struck by the lack of sharp, clear distinctions, as well as by the large measure of disagreement among the accepted authorities. Attributions of particular pieces shift, change, are challenged, or even become hyphenated. Nomenclatural practice also follows trends. For example, "Ko" is no longer stylish in many museums; originally connected with Kuan by ancient Chinese connoisseurs, and then later given, instead, a "family" relationship with Lung-ch'üan (as reputed to be the work of the elder Chang brother), it has now been deprived by many curators of any kind of independent status and completely merged into Kuan.

The very color descriptions given for most of the celadons are a maze of such locutions as: stony gray, dove gray, bluish gray, greenish gray, ash-colored, sea green, jade green, pea green, olive green, blue-green, lavender, kingfisher blue, and sky blue. (Only Northern Celadons seems to be definitely limited to one short range of hues: olive, or brownish green.) But the one color factor that is most often singled out as the optimum for a celadon is its *blueness*. And with aesthetic justice. For a celadon blue is something very special and lovely. However, if the *best* of each different type of celadon is an enchanting sky blue or blue green, it becomes even more difficult to make sound distinctions between these types with certainty.

Thus, with this general absence of common understanding among connoisseurs about just what characteristics definitely separate one celadon from another, terminology becomes somewhat more flexible than it is usually conceded to be. There are really good, technical reasons for all this. One is the basic similarity of the materials composing all these seemingly different glazes. Conversely, there is the fact that one and the same glaze may present many different colors and textures, owing to such factors as types of clay body used, adventitious variations in the mineral substance of the glaze ingredients, differing techniques in glaze application, all the shifting complexities of firing conditions, and the idiosyncrasies of the potter himself.

Coming back to my own use of attributions, then, I have tried as objectively as possible, under the circumstances, to assign my celadon glazes to name categories to which I believe them closest. My decisions have been based on much observation, study, and practice, as well as on the balancing of divergent views. In any case, for this chapter and the next, I have chosen to explain many lovely celadon glazes that represent the best of my creative efforts in this direction. Some few, of course, are off the beaten track, as I shall plainly indicate; but I have included them in this book for two good reasons: they are handsome glazes, and they are integrally related to the development of many of the other fine celadons detailed here.

Kuan-Chün

Kuan (or the "Imperial" ware made exclusively for palace use) is a kind of beautiful halfway house between Lung-ch'üan and Chün. In texture, it may have either a softly polished stone-matte surface or a brilliant, gemlike translucency; its color may vary from greenish gray to delicate light blue. (Of course, the vagaries of firing may also produce pure grays or light browns.) The limited number of glazes I have selected for this chapter all illustrate, in one way or another, these qualities of texture and color. Their differences may be attributed not only to the variations in their composition, but also to the differing methods of handling the *same* glaze for special effects. Thus, I believe the term, Kuan-Chün, to be most appropriate here; it is, incidentally, the ascription hit upon by a few authorities in their efforts to grapple with the exact designation of particular specimens of Ju, Kuan, and Chün ware.

All these glazes are closely related to CIH-p, my light blue Chün glaze in Chapter 1; all *can* have a blue color very similar to Chün; all *can* also have a very different look from Chün, one that is much closer to Kuan. And in certain cases, that "different look" will be something off on a track of its own.

CIH-m Unmilled

For a start, let me confine myself to the last-mentioned circumstance, and explain a glaze I very much value. In composition, it is *almost* identical with CIH-p, but with the exception of *one* factor; namely, the nature of the wood ashes used, as explained below in the batch recipe. The finished glaze itself is of two sorts, depending on a small variation in the method used for mixing its ingredients. One variation yields a beautiful blue-gray matte, as smooth as polished stone and (unlike true Kuan) mottled with strongly contrasting specks of rich dark brown. It is interesting to note that the more complete the reduction of the glaze, the lighter and more tactually appealing will be its color and stony texture. The other method brings us very close to actual Kuan. The speckles of dark brown disappear, and the resulting glaze is either a greenish gray or a more or less uniform soft blue-green, often with the blue predominating in some passages, the green in others; sometimes, where reduction has been counterbalanced by oxidation, the passages tend instead to soft ivory or tan. Both forms of the glaze, the Kuan-Chün type and the stony speckled matte, sometimes exhibit the tiny, dark "worm tracks" described as such in ancient Chinese descriptions of Chün. They are actually iron-rich, healed fissures created in the glaze surface fairly early in the firing and then filled in by the flow of more soluble glaze elements along their edges, just as in certain aspects of the "oil spot" glaze described in a later chapter.

The following batch recipe differs from CIH-p only in the kinds of wood ash used. Whereas the light blue Chün relies on ash exclusively from pine and spruce, the CIH-m glaze requires the same quantity of *mixed* wood ashes. That is, the ashes represent a more or less controlled burning of wood from maple, locust, birch, apple, spruce, and pine. Other combinations may successfully be tried, of course, though in every case some pine and spruce should definitely be included.

Batch Recipe		
	Buckingham feldspar	56.
	Flint	22.
	Whiting	13.
	Mixed wood ash	9.
		100.
	Yellow ochre (2.5% of batch)	2.5

Procedures for CIH-m. See the basic directions in Chapter 1 for mixing the glaze ingredients. For the blue-gray matte effect with dark brown mottlings, use the *dry-milling or sifting* method. For the uniform blue-green or the greenish gray effect, resembling Kuan, follow the *wet-milling* procedure.

Apply, dry, and fire the glaze according to the directions in Chapter 1.

Kuan-Chün and Kuan from the Same Glazes

We arrive now at a group of important glazes of related compositions that are even closer to the feel and look of their Chinese prototypes than is the one just described. All use ash only from pine and spruce, have a somewhat different formulation from the CIH glazes, and are wet-milled for about one hour.

The fired results offer a striking range of different effects which throw much light on the essential natures of Chün, Kuan, and even Ju ware glazes. Depending on such simple factors as the amount of iron present in the glaze, the placement of the ware in the kiln, and the degree of work-heat reached in the firing, these effects will grade off into each other most interestingly. Each end of the scale, as will be seen, is equally interesting and particularly significant.

CIW-p

This glaze achieves two quite different, but excellent, effects. In one, a type of Kuan frequently emerges with a soft, even-textured stony matte gray-green with a hint of blue. In the other, this "hint" becomes a frank statement: a pervading Kuan-Chün blue. (See the explanation given below under *Special Considerations*.)

Batch Recipe	Buckingham feldspar	54.
	Flint	24.
	Whiting	13.
	Softwood ash	9.
		100.
	Yellow ochre (2.5% of batch)	2.5

Gray Kuan Variant: CIW-p2

The only difference in composition of this glaze from that of the foregoing is the lessening of the amount of yellow ochre used to a mere 0.2% of the batch. This lowered iron content enables CIW-p2 to produce a fine, microcrystalline matte of a slightly blued whitish gray very close to the authentic Kuan. Thus, it is the extra iron in the CIW-p that elicits, on occasion, the entirely different qualities of a glossier texture and a soft blue Kuan-Chün color. (A fuller discussion of this phenomenon is given below under *Special Considerations*.) Another difference in the fired result is that CIW-p2 frequently develops lightly marked "worm tracks," a characteristic previously described in the discussion of CIH-m.

Use the batch recipe for CIW-p and *substitute 0.2% of yellow ochre* for the 2.5%.

CIZ-p

The basic composition of this glaze varies the proportions of the ingredients used for CIH-p even more widely than does CIW-p. As with the latter, CIZ-p exhibits the same kind of range in effects, from Kuan-Chün somewhat glossy blue to Kuan gray matte. The essential difference is that both the blue and the gray extremes are lighter and softer.

Batch Recipe	Buckingham feldspar	49.
	Flint	28.
	Whiting	14.
	Softwood ash	9.
		100.
	Yellow ochre (2.5% of batch)	2.5

Whitish Gray Kuan Variant: CIZ-p2

Here again the difference between CIZ-p and CIZ-p2 is simply the same lessened percentage of yellow ochre used in the latter: 0.2%. The result is a glaze having unusual tactile and visual appeal: a very soft matte of the finest microcrystalline structure with a lovely whitish gray Kuan color that is suffused with just the faintest suggestion of light blue. As with CIW-p2, depending on the thickness of the glaze and the degree of maturation, very fine-lined "worm tracks" are sometimes manifested.

Use the batch recipe for CIZ-p and *substitute 0.2% of yellow ochre* for the 2.5%.

Procedures for CIW-p, CIW-p2, CIZ-p, and CIZ-p2. All glazing procedures are the same as those detailed in Chapter 1. *Wet-milling* for about one hour is required for all four glazes. Application should be fairly thick, with due caution exercised, of course, to avoid extremes.

Special Considerations

Certain matters relative to these glazes require extra emphasis or additional elucidation. One is the very important question of *stacking*. Thus, for CIW-p and CIZ-p, the gray-green effect is best achieved by *not* stacking the ware in the middle levels of the kiln. Conversely, the overall blue quality that is so like Chün and, hence, Kuan-Chün, definitely requires stacking the ware in those same middle areas. For it is these portions of the kiln that assure the greatest reduction and a full cone 10 work-heat.

When we turn to CIW-p2 and CIZ-p2, we arrive at some additionally valuable insights into the way all these related glazes work out in comparison with each other. To begin with, the basic compositions of their "parent" glazes, CIW-p and CIZ-p, are both more refractory when fired than is CIH-p, having a eutectic range that starts and goes somewhat higher than the latter. In turn, CIW-p2 and CIZ-p2 are both even more refractory than CIW-p and CIZ-p, with a eutectic that *begins* at cone 10; at cone 9, they are still relatively immature. As has been made clear in the introductory descriptions of each glaze, there is a vast difference in appearance between each parent glaze and its variant. And it is significant that the whole range of differences is exactly parallel throughout the related family of Chün and Kuan-Chün glazes. Thus, for example, the least refractory composition is the wet-milled form of the light blue Chün, CIH-p, which reaches some degree of maturation anywhere in a cone 10 reduction firing. So it should be no surprise that CIH-p, like the Kuan-Chün glazes, moves that much closer to Kuan when it too has its yellow ochre percentage appreciably reduced below its usual 2.5% of the batch.

The foregoing adds up to the clear fact that, over and above the varying eutectics produced by different proportions among the basic glaze components, like silica and feldspar, the role of *iron* is vital to these differing effects. It is the increased or decreased fluxing and tinctorial powers of iron that shift the qualities of glaze in one direction or the other, toward light blue Chün or, conversely, toward whitish gray Kuan. The simple principle here, within exactly prescribed limits, of course, is: the more iron in the glaze, the more Chün-like it will be; the less iron, the more Kuan-like. It is perhaps needless to add that we are speaking, in this connection, only of glazes of the CIH-p through the CIZ-p2 range. For certain other, entirely different compositions, it is important to realize that extra increments of iron would merely move the total glaze effect closer to the *brownish* appearance of, say, a Northern Celadon.

A final point about the impact of iron on eutectics and color: we should not forget the fact that the color of the clay body used for the ware itself will markedly influence the glaze effect. Any clay body rich in iron will therefore tend to contribute to the glaze qualities more like Kuan-Chün and less like Kuan. (See Chapter 11 for information on clay bodies.)

3
OTHER VARIETIES OF CELADON

This chapter is a logical extension of the previous one and encompasses most of the other varieties of celadons I have developed. Once again, it would be possible to cavil at the choice of category I assign to each. But, as I have already explained, celadon categories are far from airtight. Just as in the previous chapter, what matters most is that each celadon glaze presented here is a formulation of practical value to the serious potter, as well as a likely source of enlightenment to the connoisseur and the collector. The many glazes that make up this chapter more or less grade into each other, from those resembling Lung-ch'üan to those closer to Kuan, Ko, Northern Celadon, Ju, and Koryo. Most are within the boundaries of Sung dynasty quality; a few wander out of or into other provenances.

Lung-ch'üan

From among the many glazes I have developed which I assign to Lung-ch'üan, I have selected seven for the first major subdivision of the present chapter. Four of these depart from the pattern of composition thus far exemplified in this book in that they omit wood ash as an ingredient, and approach celadon-making on entirely different bases. The other three represent a combined approach, either using wood ash or blending among themselves with or without wood ash. Their colors range from gray and gray-greens of varying intensities to light bluish greens. In texture, they vary from translucent to semi-opaque.

Lung-Ch'üan Formulas and Recipes: High-Lime Types

The parent of this first group is a reconstruction I first made of a glaze quoted by Parmelee (see *Bibliography*) from H.W. Nichols under the heading of "ancient Chinese glaze." (It was not until many years later that I realized that the particular Chinese glaze Nichols had analyzed was, in fact, a very early proto-porcelain type found rather sparsely covering a few Han dynasty pots collected by Berthold Laufer [see *Bibliography*]. It was therefore a glaze antedating Sung times and major Lung-ch'üan activity by well over 750 years.) Having created an empirical formula and then a batch recipe from this chemical analysis, I dubbed the resulting glaze "ACG" and at once plunged into variations on it.

ACGW-H1

One of the most interesting of these variations at first proved to be a totally unfamiliar, satiny smooth, fine-grained matte of soft ivory white hue when fired at cone 8 in *oxidation*; in this state, it had no resemblance to any celadon whatsoever. Yet when fired to cones 9 or 10 with heavy *reduction*, the same glaze produced a pale gray celadon of a somewhat translucent Ch'ing dynasty appearance, rather than that of earlier periods. Its composition is remarkable in that it has not only a significant amount of magnesium, but unusually large proportions of lime and kaolin. This fact is very much in keeping with Nichols' statement that the glaze is essentially a mixture of a proto-porcelain body clay and a good amount of limestone.

Empirical Formula	.7572 CaO	.375 Al_2O_3	2.2316 SiO_2
	.1135 MgO		
	.1291 K_2O		

Batch Recipe		
	Whiting	75.72
	Magnesium carbonate	9.53
	Buckingham feldspar	76.94
	Georgia kaolin	59.13
	Flint	56.43
		277.75

ACGW1-FK1: A Variant with Iron Silicate

The preceding glaze may be brought closer to the light green of a true Lung-ch'üan by the addition of various iron oxides. For example, one interesting green celadon effect is achieved by the addition of iron silicate, a colorant employed by the Japanese research-er, Ishii. This colorant consists of one part of red iron oxide mixed with three parts of flint, which is then reduction fired to cone 10, and finally ground without water in a mortar, or in a ball mill, to a fine powder. Two percent of this colorant mix added to the glaze batch recipe of ACGW-H1 helps produce a delicate, light green celadon.

ACGW4-F3

This is one of the most satisfactory glazes in our group of high-lime, Lung-ch'üan-type celadons. When fully reduced at cone 10, it is a beautifully translucent but cloudy bluish green; at cones 8 and 9, it verges into a soft matte of the same hue. (On occasion, I should add, I have sometimes achieved an enriching of the color by super-imposing on the already applied glaze a faint overspray of the light blue Chün glaze, CIH-p, in the wet-milled form.) As will be noted in the following empirical formula, the only difference from ACGW-H1 is the increased silica; the result is actually a *lowered* eutectic point. In the batch recipe, a small amount of iron oxide is also added.

Empirical Formula	.7572 CaO	.375 Al_2O_3	2.85 SiO_2
	.1135 MgO		
	.1291 K_2O		

Batch Recipe		
Whiting		75.72
Magnesium carbonate		9.53
Buckingham feldspar		76.94
Georgia kaolin		59.13
Flint		93.44
		314.76
Black iron oxide (1.0% of batch)		3.14

ACG8

Here we have a glaze that more or less belongs in the same high-lime family of celadons, but it also departs from the preceding glazes in several respects. It shifts the balance between lime and feldspar, each about 24% in ACGW4-F3, so that there is 7% less lime and 12% more feldspar. Equally important, it adds wood ash to the list of components. No colorant is added. The resulting celadon is light in color and slightly opaque, tending somewhat toward a whiter gray-green with an attractive, rather unctuous look and feel. It has a wide firing range, being effective at all levels of the kiln in a cone 10 firing. (Only the batch recipe is given below, since the presence of wood ash would render an empirical formula much too conjectural.)

Batch Recipe		
Whiting		17.
Magnesium carbonate		2.
Buckingham feldspar		36.
Georgia kaolin		12.
Flint		27.
Softwood ash		6.
		100.

Procedures for ACGW-H1, ACGW1-FK1, ACGW4-F3, and ACG8. All mixing, applying, drying, and firing procedures are the same as those detailed in Chapter 1. All these glazes require wet-milling for about one hour. Because of the relatively large proportions of clay used in their composition, be careful to use as little water as possible in applying to the ware, so as to prevent the formation of hairline cracks as the glaze begins to dry. Otherwise, the fired pots will almost certainly show unseemly crawling and brownish bare spots. For the same reason, regardless of how much or how little water is in the glaze mix, do not overwet the bisque with excessively thick application.

Lung-Ch'üan: Basic Granite Powder Type

We now turn to a glaze that represents a complete departure in composition from those in the group just described. It also creates the basis for a wide variety of other glaze combinations, some of which are detailed in both this and the following chapter. The special nature of this glaze derives from the use of a particular material with which I have done much experimentation. It is a granite powder I first obtained many years ago through the kindness of Mr. E.F. Wall of the Wells-Lamson Quarry Company at Barre, Vermont, together with a chemical analysis of it. Granites vary considerably in composition, a fact that can be put to good use in ceramics. From Barre, however, I had a sufficient supply of a stable material with which to achieve a number of quite desirable results.

The percentage analysis supplied me by Mr. Wall was:

SiO_2	70.0 %
Al_2O_3	15.35%
CaO	2.0 %
Na_2O	5.2 %
K_2O	4.45%
Fe_2O_3	2.0 %
L.O.I.	1.0 %

From this I derived the following empirical:

.2835 K_2O	.9016 Al_2O_3	6.9904 SiO_2
.214 CaO	.0749 Fe_2O_3	
.5023 Na_2O		

It is evident that the granite powder with which I have worked, then, is comparable to a soda feldspar. The chief difference is the hematite contained in the granite powder, an ingredient which furnishes one of the forms of iron (Fe_2O_3) so essential to the producing of celadons. Another important difference is the presence in the granite powder of a significant amount of CaO (lime), as compared with the negligible amount in the usual kind of marketed soda feldspar.

G#6

This is probably one of the best celadons among a dozen or so I have developed with this granite powder (not counting those made in combination with other glaze types). Fired with heavy reduction to cone 10, it becomes a rich, dark, gray-green color with semi-opaque texture. (A lighter, faintly mottled, oatmeal tan is produced at cones 8 and 9 in a moderately reducing fire.) Like the basic ACG glazes, this composition dispenses with wood ash and yet possesses great depth. As will be seen later, it also combines well with other glaze compositions that do contain wood ash, and thus serves importantly in the creation of several additional glazes of beauty and distinction.

Empirical Formula	.0785 K_2O	.3497 Al_2O_3	4.115 SiO_2
	.7824 CaO	.0207 Fe_2O_3	
	.1391 Na_2O		

Batch Recipe	Granite powder	166.01
	Whiting	72.32
	Georgia kaolin	25.8
	Flint	118.65
		382.78

Procedures for G#6. Follow the directions for mixing, applying, drying, and firing given in Chapter 1. Wet-milling for no more than one hour is required.

Lung-Ch'üan: Combined Formulations

The two remaining Lung-ch'üan glazes explained in this section offer a deepening of the blueness in the celadon effect, as well as an increased unctuosity of surface. Each represents two distinct types of combined glaze formulations.

CEL#4

In origin, this glaze is a blend of two previously explained compositions, ACGW4-F3 and CIH-m, with the former contributing about five-sixths of the total. It is therefore a high-lime celadon rendered more feldspathic and further enriched with wood ash. It produces a good, faintly bluish, green celadon.

Batch Recipe		
	Buckingham feldspar	104.94
	Whiting	82.22
	Magnesium carbonate	9.53
	Georgia kaolin	59.13
	Mixed-wood ash	4.5
	Flint	104.44
	Black iron oxide	3.14
	Yellow ochre	1.25
		369.15

CEL#6

This combination glaze brings together differing proportions of variants of two other glazes already described, one related to G#6 and the other to CIH-p. Both parent glazes, however, contain definite deviations in composition from these two. Among other things, in one case Maine feldspar is substituted for Buckingham feldspar; and in the other, lithium is introduced as an ingredient. (According to a reference cited by Hetherington, lithium has been identified by spectroscopic analysis as a component of some Sung celadons.) The resulting glaze is a markedly blue-green celadon which, at its best, has great depth and an unctuous tactile appeal.

Batch Recipe		
	Granite powder	82.14
	Maine feldspar	112.0
	Whiting	57.16
	Lithium carbonate	3.7
	Georgia kaolin	12.9
	Flint	103.32
	Softwood ash	18.0
	Yellow ochre	5.0
		394.22

Procedures for CEL#4 and CEL#6. Follow the directions for mixing, applying, drying, and firing given in Chapter 1. Wet-mill for no more than three-quarters of an hour. In application, be careful to achieve the mean between the extremes of excessive thinness or excessive thickness. The former will lose the blue depth of the glaze's potential; the latter will cause an excess of small, entrapped bubbles, forming a sort of unsightly froth in areas of the glaze when fired. Excessive milling of the glaze mixture will produce the same phenomenon.

Kuan

In this section, I have chosen to describe glazes that closely resemble certain varieties of Kuan, particularly those that tend to remain uncrazed. (Crackle glazes, or Ko-type Kuan, I reserve for a later section of this chapter.) Depending on the vagaries of firing, many of these glazes develop a blue quality of such intensity that they come close to Chün or lap over into the conjectural Ju, the same phenomenon I have already remarked on in Chapter 2. Most frequently, however, they represent those Kuan types that have either a whitish gray or a delicate blue-green coloration. The textures vary from unctuous or stony matte to semi-opaques of different degrees of translucency.

Such overlappings of characteristics and types should not be too surprising to anyone familiar with the literature on Sung glazes. For example, Basil Gray notes that "Kuan pieces have a wide range of colour," listing them as going from "watery green" through an "intense lavender blue" and "gray blue" to a "whitish glaze." And elsewhere he remarks that a particular variety of "Chün products" described as having been "made for the scholar's table [water pots, shallow dishes, and small boxes], may be deemed to have set the line for the later classic wares of Kuan and Ko." Finally, Sir Harry Garner says that "what is generally known as Kinuta celadon," a bluish variety of Lung-ch'üan, "may have a colour almost indistinguishable from that of a Kuan piece of high quality." Such observations are fully supported by my practical experience in formulating and firing Sung-type glazes that answer to virtually the same descriptions.

Kuan with Whitish Matte Glazes

To continue from the point where we left the matter at the end of Chapter 2, we shall now resume with the whiter, more matte Kuan types. It will be remembered that we reserved for the final entry in that chapter a remarkably smooth, stony, whitish gray glaze with a hint of blue, CIZ-p2. We might just as logically have reserved it for a first entry here; it was only its family connection with the other glazes in that chapter that determined its placement there. The next glaze is also a smooth, stony matte, but its composition resembles those in the preceding Lung-ch'üan section.

CEL#16

In its best form, this Kuan is a whitish gray with a faint tinge of green. Its surface is exactly like that of a fine-grained, softly polished stone. These qualities can be achieved most consistently by careful attention to the procedures for applying and firing indicated below. A quite different effect consisting of a very light, delicate blue translucency is produced by following other procedures also explained below.

The ingredients listed in the batch recipe below place this glaze squarely in the same family of compositions as CEL#6. The basic differences are the marked increase of feldspar in substitution for granite powder, the mixture of soda feldspar with potash feldspar, and the replacement of the softwood ash by the mixed-wood variety. The fired results, of course, are quite different from those of the related glaze.

Batch Recipe	Granite powder	45.38
	Maine feldspar	66.19
	Buckingham feldspar	81.00
	Whiting	58.48
	Lithium carbonate	3.70
	Georgia kaolin	12.47
	Flint	103.82
	Mixed-wood ash	18.00
	Yellow ochre	2.50
		391.54

Procedures for CEL#16. Follow the directions for mixing, applying, drying, and firing given in Chapter 1. Wet-mill for no more than one hour.

For the whitish gray matte effect, apply *thickly* to the ware. For the light blue translucent effect, first apply a coating of white slip (see Chapter 11 for recipe) to the greenware at the leatherhard stage before bisquing the ware; then apply a thin-to-medium-thick coating of the glaze.

Placement in the kiln is of critical importance. In a cone 10 firing, the whitish matte results are best achieved in the upper and lower levels of the kiln. Blue effects, both with and without white slip, require placement in the middle levels of greatest heat and reduction.

SKA

This is another matte, but with a very different, much more unctuous quality. The color is an exceptionally soft, milky whitish gray with the green tinge veering more toward blue than in the case of the preceding glaze. The general effect strikes me as being a sort of "moon glow" of great tactile appeal. Its potential for crazing under certain circumstances would put it, perhaps, in the class of Ko or crackle-type Kuan (presented later in this chapter). However, I include it here because with careful firing controls it need not craze.

The glaze composition is remarkably simple, using a very large proportion of feldspar. The wood ash adds significantly to its texture.

Batch Recipe	Buckingham feldspar	80.
	Whiting	7.
	Flint	7.
	Softwood ash	6.
		100.

Procedures for SKA. Follow the directions for mixing, applying, drying, and firing given in Chapter 1. Wet-milling is required for no more than one hour. Application should be fairly thick. For the uncrazed effect, placement in the kiln should be in the middle levels, and the glaze should be given the fullest maturation and reduction at cone 10.

Blue-Green Kuan

We come now to those varieties of Kuan that veer away completely from the whitish gray mattes to the relatively translucent blue-greens. As has been remarked before, there is really no hard-and-fast dividing line in glaze characteristics between a fine blue-green Kuan and a fine blue-green Lung-ch'üan. Indeed, the so-called "Kinuta" variety of the latter fits this general description so well that certain Lung-ch'üan pieces have been considered in some quarters as direct imitations of Kuan. Which brings us full circle.

Call them what one will, the group of four related glazes concluding this section are very attractive blue-green celadons. Each of them is almost identical in composition with the Lung-ch'üan CEL#6, the only differences being the degree to which soda feldspar is substituted for potash feldspar and the type of wood ash employed. The group demonstrates how a progression of subtle changes in the finished glazes can be achieved by delicate readjustments of one basic formulation.

CEL#7

An exceptionally attractive blue-green of very subtle texture, this glaze is bluest where it is thickest, owing in part to the opalescence created by the entrapment of a multitude of very tiny bubbles in its structure. I consider it one of my finest celadons.

Batch Recipe		
	Granite powder	82.14
	Buckingham feldspar	50.0
	Maine feldspar	62.0
	Whiting	57.16
	Lithium carbonate	3.7
	Georgia kaolin	12.9
	Flint	103.32
	Softwood ash	18.0
	Yellow ochre	5.0
		394.22

CEL#11

The only difference between the formulations of this and the immediately preceding glaze is the substitution of mixed-wood ash for the softwood type. Somewhat less bubbly in structure, the fired glaze has even a closer texture and a rich celadon color with a delicate, light sky-blue cast. The somewhat lighter blue tones here are probably attributable to the use of the mixed-wood ash.

Batch Recipe	Granite powder	82.14
	Buckingham feldspar	50.0
	Maine feldspar	62.0
	Whiting	57.16
	Lithium carbonate	3.7
	Georgia kaolin	12.9
	Flint	103.32
	Mixed-wood ash	18.0
	Yellow ochre	5.0
		394.22

CEL#14

Here the blue effect is somewhat deeper than it is in CEL#11. Using the mixed-wood ash, it changes the balance of feldspar towards much potash feldspar.

Batch Recipe	Granite powder	82.14
	Buckingham feldspar	81.0
	Maine feldspar	31.0
	Whiting	57.16
	Lithium carbonate	3.7
	Georgia kaolin	12.9
	Flint	103.32
	Mixed-wood ash	18.0
	Yellow ochre	5.0
		394.22

CEL#13

The final celadon in both this group and the Kuan section has darker hues than its foregoing relatives, thereby bringing it rather close to the Koryo type explored in the next section of this chapter. The wood ash used here is pine, and the balance between the soda and potash feldspars represents yet another adjustment. The fired glaze has a tendency to delayed crazing, a quality suggesting a possible alignment with Ko crackle type glazes.

Batch Recipe	Granite powder	82.14
	Buckingham feldspar	71.0
	Maine feldspar	41.0
	Whiting	57.16
	Lithium carbonate	3.7
	Georgia kaolin	12.9
	Flint	103.32
	Softwood ash	18.0
	Yellow ochre	5.0
		394.22

Procedures for CEL#7, CEL#11, CEL#14, and CEL#13. Follow the directions for mixing, applying, drying, and firing given in Chapter 1. Wet-milling for no more than three-quarters of an hour is required for each of these glazes. Avoid too thick or too thin an application to the ware.

In the case of CEL#11, a very delicate, somewhat more grayed effect may be obtained by first applying white slip (see Chapter 11 for recipe) to the leatherhard greenware, bisquing the ware, and then applying the glaze.

Best bluish colorations are achieved in the middle levels of the kiln with full reduction at cone 10.

Koryo

A major achievement of Korean ceramics, the Koryo celadon glaze obviously seems to have been very much influenced in its development by Chinese celadons. Though the initial impetus may have derived from the Yüeh celadons spanning several early Chinese dynasties, the closest resemblances can be seen between Koryo and the more or less contemporary achievements in Sung dynasty China. As remarked by Gompertz in his fine book on Korean celadons (see *Bibliography*),"In general, the Koryo celadon glaze resembles that of the well-known Lung-ch'üan celadons." Elsewhere in the same book, he states, "From whatever angle we view the matter, the resemblance between Koryo celadons . . . and the ware now identified as Ju is quite astonishing," adding that it is "easy at first glance to mistake" one for the other, though "the hint of lavender" in some Ju ware might serve to distinguish them. Another investigator, Nomori, is cited by Gompertz as having identified 65 different shades of Koryo glaze color, ranging "from gray to dark brown through every kind of blue, green, and olive."

But in the interests of simplification, let us return to the concept of the *optimum* Koryo qualities. What are they? By now it should come as no surprise that here, too (as Gompertz puts it), "those with a light bluish colour are the finest, followed by those with bluish green." Or as expressed by W.B. Honey (see *Bibliography*) "the Corean ware at its best has a characteristic very smooth bluish grey-green glaze," noting also the resemblance at times to the legendary "bluish-green Chinese Ju ware."

The range of texture goes from a soft semi-matte through slightly less opaque consistencies to a cloudy, semi-translucent structure of great depth. As in the case of parallel Chinese glazes, the more or less cloudy quality, as well as the bluish tints, is owing partly to tiny, undissolved particles of glaze ingredients, partly to the close-packed, minute bubbles captured in the matrix and produced, in turn, mainly by the phosphorus-releasing wood ash in the glaze mixture.

I have reserved four glazes, belonging to three different types of formulation, for this section.

KCC#3

This celadon is very close to my idea of a really good Koryo glaze. It is a rich, medium-light green, usually with a strong suggestion of blue created, in part, by a very finely textured mass of extremely tiny bubbles. This suggestion becomes a pervading cloud of jade blue when the glaze is applied to the optimum thickness. Fully reduced and matured, it possesses a matrix of great depth and unctuousness. In addition, like one variety of semi-translucent Koryo, it builds up thickly in the depressions and crevices made by carved designs and cup-handle connections, creating the impression of some handsomely congealed liquid substance.

It will be noted that its formulation belongs to the same family as the Chün and Kuan-Chün glazes, but the proportions involved are quite different.

Batch Recipe		
	Buckingham feldspar	66.
	Georgia kaolin	4.
	Whiting	8.
	Flint	12.
	Softwood ash	10.
		100.
	Yellow ochre (1.66% of batch)	1.66

Procedures for KCC#3. Follow the directions given in Chapter 1 for mixing this glaze, *but with the following caution:* to insure the color and texture described above, this glaze should be wet-milled only from one-half to three-quarters of an hour, no more. Excessive milling will unquestionably destroy the optimum effect and, instead, will produce an uneven, bumpy surface marred by numerous large bubbles and aggregations of assorted smaller ones that look like vitrified froth — in sum, a vastly unsatisfactory result as compared to the delicate softness of the correctly milled glaze.

For applying, drying, and firing, follow the directions given in Chapter 1. Avoid the opposite extremes of thickness in applying the glaze. For uncrazed results, fire the ware in the middle levels of the kiln at cone 10.

CH+CX

Here too is a richly textured, semi-translucent, blue-green glaze of much depth. As will be noted, its composition is more or less related to a number of the Kuan glazes described in the previous section.

Batch Recipe		
	Buckingham feldspar	28.0
	Maine feldspar	23.5
	Granite powder	15.0
	Whiting	12.0
	Flint	17.0
	Softwood ash	4.5
		100.0
	Yellow ochre (1.25% of batch)	1.25

Procedures for CH+CX. Follow the directions for mixing, applying, drying, and firing given in Chapter 1. For best results, it is advisable to make up fresh batches for application during a relatively limited period of time. Wet-mill for about three-quarters of an hour. Application of the glaze to the ware should be thick. Use the middle levels of the kiln in a cone 10 firing.

SKA-F2

The major and only difference between this simple glaze and the formulation of the SKA glaze described under Kuan is the addition of a very small amount of iron oxide. But the difference as seen in the fired results is vast. The color tones jump from the Kuan milky whitish gray to a very authentic-looking Koryo blue-green that ranges in texture from a glossy translucent to a more unctuous semi-opaque with a slightly grayed cast. By this point in our book, the quality of color induced by iron in high-feldspathic glazes should be no surprise; the phenomenon is implicit in a good number of the glazes I have already described, many of them quite rich in feldspar of one type or another, or in combination. In the case of SKA-F2, there is just one feldspar in high concentration. And, of course, the iron is there to bring out the color. The rich texture and the special color qualities are emphasized by the softwood ash.

Batch Recipe		
	Buckingham feldspar	80.
	Whiting	7.
	Flint	7.
	Softwood ash	6.
		100.
	Black iron oxide (1.0% of batch)	1.

Procedures for SKA-F2. Follow the directions for mixing, applying, drying, and firing given in Chapter 1. Wet-mill for about one hour. For grayer, more opaque effects, stack the ware in the lower levels of the kiln; for greater blueness and translucency, use the middle levels.

SK-F2

Even simpler in composition than the preceding glaze, this one is obviously of the same generic type. The major difference here is the omission of the wood ash. The fired result, in its more translucent forms, is something that might almost be dubbed a Ch'ing dynasty-type Koryo, an improbable name, of course, from the historical stand-point. However, at its best it is a beautiful glaze of Koryo color, a strongly blue celadon green with an excellent, lustrous finish. When matured to just the right point and not overfired, its surface and color approximate more exactly the true Koryo contemporary with Sung times. Ironically, this glaze was inspired by a plain white Shino glaze formulation given in Sanders' book on Japanese ceramics (see *Bibliography*), a glaze effect that seems worlds away from Koryo celadon.

I should add that the omission of the wood ash, though it seems to intensify the blueness of the glaze in this case, somewhat diminishes the unctuous quality found in SK-F2.

Batch Recipe		
	Buckingham feldspar	83.
	Whiting	9.
	Flint	8.
		100.
	Black iron oxide (1.5% of batch)	1.5

Procedures for SK-F2. Follow the directions for mixing, applying, drying, and firing given in Chapter 1. Wet-mill for about one hour. Stack ware as indicated above under SKA-F2. Probably the best stacking level is halfway between the middle and the floor of the kiln.

Northern Celadon

The class of celadons traditionally called "Northern" is typified by a darker, browner coloration and by an often glassier texture. In Sung ceramics, it was habitually used with carved, incised, or molded surfaces. Filling the indentations and declivities, it brought out the beauty of the floral designs, thereby emphasizing their three-dimensionality. In this respect, the Northern Celadons closely resemble many of the richly carved Koryo pieces, though the typical colors and textures in each provenance are quite different.

Of the many glazes of this type, I have selected from my formulations five representative specimens. In composition, most are related to each other and to glazes in previous sections. The first three form one group for which the handling procedures are the same.

ACGW1-FK6

This is the same glaze as the variant ACGW1-FK1 described in the Lung-ch'üan section, but with extra additions of the iron silicate colorant. To create the olive green Northern Celadon effect, the amount of iron silicate has been tripled.

Batch Recipe		
	Whiting	75.72
	Magnesium carbonate	9.53
	Buckingham feldspar	76.94
	Georgia kaolin	59.13
	Flint	56.43
		277.75
	Iron silicate (6% of batch)	16.67

ACG-L1

Here, too, ACGW-H1 is the jumping-off point for the formulation of a dark, olive green celadon. In this case, lithium (via spodumene) is included as a partial substitution for the lime, as well as for some of the flint. Again, 6% of the iron silicate is employed.

Empirical Formula			
	$.6572\ CaO$	$.375\ Al_2O_3$	$2.2316\ SiO_2$
	$.1135\ MgO$		
	$.1291\ K_2O$		
	$.1\quad Li_2O$		

Batch Recipe		
	Whiting	65.72
	Magnesium carbonate	9.53
	Buckingham feldspar	76.94

	Spodumene	37.2
	Georgia kaolin	33.33
	Flint	44.43
		267.15
	Iron silicate (6% of batch)	16.03

ACG7-F4

As is so often the case, the presence of wood ash in this olive green glaze produces a somewhat richer texture with good depth that effectively emphasizes carved decorative treatment of the ware.

Batch Recipe	Whiting	22.
	Magnesium carbonate	3.
	Buckingham feldspar	23.
	Georgia kaolin	18.
	Flint	28.
	Softwood ash	6.
		100.
	Black iron oxide (1.5% of batch)	1.5

Procedures for ACGW1-FK6, ACG-L1, and ACG7-F4. Follow the directions for mixing, applying, drying, and firing given in Chapter 1. Wet-mill for about one hour. Use as little water as possible in applying to the ware so as to avoid hairline cracks and crawling in the later stages. Avoid excessively thick application for the same reasons.

CEL#3

This is another Northern Celadon with a rich dark color and great depth. Though it contains the same materials that make up the Lung-ch'üan CEL#4, it utilizes them in very different proportions.

Batch Recipe	Whiting	57.36
	Magnesium carbonate	4.76
	Buckingham feldspar	122.47
	Georgia kaolin	29.56
	Flint	79.72
	Black iron oxide	1.53
	Yellow ochre	5.37
		314.27

Procedures for CEL#3. Follow the directions for mixing, applying, drying, and firing given in Chapter 1. Wet-mill for about one hour.

KCC#6

I have reserved for final place in this section a handsome glaze that might be called a halfway house between Northern Celadon and Koryo. It is a deep olive green with a smooth, rich texture of some unctuosity, especially when it is thickly applied. The matrix is filled with a mass of uniformly minute bubbles. Its color is darkened and its opacity increased both by thickness of application and placement in the lower levels of the kiln.

Batch Recipe		
	Maine feldspar	43.0
	Georgia kaolin	8.7
	Whiting	11.5
	Flint	26.8
	Softwood ash	10.0
		100.0
	Yellow ochre (1.66% of batch)	1.66

Procedures for KCC#6. Follow the directions for mixing, drying, applying, and firing given in Chapter 1. Wet-mill for no more than three-quarters of an hour to avoid excessive, uneven bubbling in the fired glaze. For darker color and increased opacity, apply the glaze thickly and/or place the ware in the lower levels of the kiln. The converse effects of lighter color and increased translucency require thinner glaze application and/or placement of ware in the middle levels of the kiln.

Ko (or Crackled Kuan)

In the past, most dark-crackled celadons of Chinese Sung provenance have often been given the attribution of "Ko" ware. Historically, the term is somewhat confusing. Originally, it was applied to the celadons produced by the legendary elder Chang, one of two brothers who were said to have produced pottery in the Lung-ch'üan neighborhood during the Southern Sung period. (The younger brother's pottery, in contradistinction, was said to be the uncrackled variety of Lung-ch'üan celadon.) Later, the term "Ko" was applied to *Kuan* ware of the crackled type, and, in fact, to any Sung celadon of darkly defined crackled pattern. Most recent scholarship tends to consider Ko a crackled variety of Kuan. Like the latter, it is often a richly bubbled glaze resembling those types of uncrackled Kuan that possess relatively more opacity and a polished-stone texture. All of this is in keeping with the understandable confusion in attribution between Kuan and Lung-ch'üan bluish green celadons, especially when certain pieces are identified as Lung-ch'üan imitations of crackled Kuan!

Causes of Crackle

In any case, crackle is essentially the same thing as crazing, the only difference being that the cracks in the glaze are more or less controlled and encouraged, or, if accidental, exploited for decorative purposes. Crazing is caused by the different rates of expansion and contraction of a glaze as compared with those of the body of the ware it encases. It may occur immediately after a firing, it may suddenly manifest itself hours later, or it may slowly develop over a much longer period of time, sometimes years. Changes in temperature and humidity normally produce such expansion and contraction in all ware, and crazing can be totally avoided only if these factors are in a similar ratio in both glaze and body.

The chemical composition of each (body and glaze) determines the ratio. Highly alkaline glazes, for example, have an inherent tendency to craze, no matter what body they are applied to; such crazing is almost inevitable. Glazes rich in feldspar also have something of the same tendency, though very much less; but in their case, the tendency is offset and even canceled by several other factors. These can be: (1) increased proportions of silica in either the glaze or the body; (2) a significant amount of reduction during the firing process, which dissolves more of the body surface, and thereby lessens the strains between body and glaze; and (3) the achievement of the optimum work-heats required in firing a given type of ware.

The *prevention* of crazing, of course, is not what we are concerned with in this section of our book. Rather, the question here becomes how to *encourage* craze patterns that will lend themselves to the decorative quality known as "crackle." In part, the answer is that, for high-feldspathic glazes of the Ko type, the basic approach is to utilize glaze compositions which include very large amounts of feldspar and proportionally less flint. Similarly, the body should contain somewhat less flint than would be required for an uncrackled glaze effect.

The staining of crackle is explained at the end of this section.

COX#1

This first formulation yields a smooth, stony gray celadon with a large crackle very much like the pattern described as "crab's claw." It is based on a "siltstone" glaze developed and reported by Paul E. Cox (see *Bibliography*) many years ago.

Batch Recipe		
	Granite powder	29.75
	Maine feldspar	47.31
	Whiting	11.33
	Flint	11.61
		100.00

KCC#3 (as Crackle Glaze)

The batch recipe for the second glaze here has already been given in the earlier section on Koryo. A rich blue-green celadon of somewhat glossy texture when normally fired to full maturity at cone 10, it can maintain a smooth, uncrazed surface without any change through the years. However, when fired to about cone 9, it develops a slowly forming craze which can be converted to a handsome, large crackle pattern. The color is darker and the texture much "fattier" than the same glaze at the higher maturation point. The crackle is widest and most handsome when the glaze is applied to stoneware Body #4. (See Chapter 11 for clay body recipes.)

Batch Recipe		
	Buckingham feldspar	66.
	Georgia kaolin	4.
	Whiting	8.
	Flint	12.
	Softwood ash	10.
		100.0
	Yellow ochre (1.66% of batch)	1.66

KCC#3b: A Variant of KCC#3

In composition, this is simply the same glaze as KCC#3 *without* the yellow ochre colorant. Fired to about cone 9, it develops a very slow craze which, with the technique of "encouragement" explained in the final part of this section, becomes a good stained crackle. Its crackle pattern tends to be smaller spaced than that of the regular KCC#3. Its color is closer to many specimens of Ko-type Kuan, being a very light gray-green. It should be noted, however, that when it is fired to cone 10, no craze appears, and in fact none can be induced (at least on the ware bodies I customarily employ).

Follow the batch recipe given above for KCC#3, but *omit the yellow ochre completely*.

SK#1

Here we have a cone 8 to cone 9 reduction glaze which runs toward white rather than toward celadon, especially at the lower cone. Like COX#1 and the other uncombined granite-powder glazes, it dispenses with wood ash, but it is even simpler in composition. The crackle patterns it produces are very wide-spaced on some pieces, and its pure white opacity creates a strong contrast with the stained crackle marks. As previously noted in the Koryo section, it is a modification of a Shino glaze reported by Sanders.

Batch Recipe		
	Buckingham feldspar	83.
	Whiting	9.
	Flint	8.
		100.0

SKA (as Crackle Glaze)

Again we have a repetition of a glaze composition, this time one already detailed in an earlier section of this chapter under Kuan. There, you may recall, I noted its potential for crazing. At slightly over cone 9, it produces, with encouragement, very large patterns that take very dark staining which are all the more appealing against the light gray "moon glow" quality of the glaze itself. At cone 9 or slightly less, the patterns are smaller-spaced and less boldly stained. Either effect is quite handsome.

Batch Recipe		
	Buckingham feldspar	80.
	Whiting	7.
	Flint	7.
	Softwood ash	6.
		100.0

Crackle from Glaze Combinations

Finally, certain combinations of glaze in the form of one lightly sprayed over the other on a given piece will produce large, interesting crackle effects. A particularly good combination, creating a rich, blue celadon color broken up by large crackle patterns that stain rather well, is CIH-m sprayed over CEL#7. (See Chapters 2 and 3, respectively, for the batch recipes of these two.) The basic glaze, CEL#7, should first be applied fairly thick; the CIH-m should then be sprayed in a somewhat thin but even layer directly on top of the CEL#7. After being fired, the ware can be hurried along to a handsome crackle by means of the procedures described below under *Techniques for Staining Crackle.*

Procedures for Crackle Glazes. Follow the directions for mixing, applying, and drying given in Chapter 1. COX#1, KCC#3, and KCC#3b should be made up fresh for use within a limited period of time. SK#1 and SKA are more stable, and the same batches can be used over longer periods. Mill for only three-quarters of an hour.

Avoid applying COX#1 too thickly, so as to prevent uneven, overlarge bubbling in the glaze texture. The others can be applied in moderately thick coatings more safely, however.

For firing, follow the directions given in Chapter 1, *with the following special cautions:* It is especially important that the ware be placed in the cooler, rather than the hottest, parts of the kiln so that the glaze may reach a maturation point somewhat below its full potential. For the crackle effect, it is better to err on the slightly *under*fired side than on the *over*fired side, since the resulting matte or semi-matte surface, when crazed, holds the crackle-defining stains much better than does one with a high gloss. Thus, the lower and upper levels of the kiln are preferable to the middle ones for the crackle effect.

There is, to be sure, a kind of crazing that is induced by *over*firing, but it is much less desirable for staining into crackle patterns. Many of the feldspathic glazes described in this book can be made to craze either by overfiring or underfiring, especially on certain bodies. For example, the light blue Chün, CIH-p, will craze when overfired, but the resulting glossy surface does not take staining as well as do the glazes specified above in this section.

Techniques for Staining Crackle

The best staining material I have found is Chinese ink, either in stick or liquid form. In the stick form, the ink is first prepared by rubbing it on an unglazed stoneware slab or dish in a tiny amount of water. Either form of ink is then applied by brush to the surface of the already crazed ware. Before applying the ink, whether you use the methods of inducing craze indicated below or not, be sure the ware is thoroughly warmed through so as to expand the craze lines for easier access to the ink.

The large crackle pattern in a feldspathic glaze normally develops at a rather slow rate after the firing is over, but it can be hurried along to the desired stage by alternate immersions of the fired ware in very cold and very hot water. In some instances, I have even resorted to a kind of "torture treatment": quick changes back and forth several times between ice water or snow and rapidly boiling water! If both body and glaze are well composed and correctly fired, no dunting occurs, and a good craze pattern begins to develop. Some ware may require several such treatments before sufficient crazing takes place. In some cases, these treatments must be spaced out over several days or even weeks. In time, though, and with patient repetition of the "torture" technique, you will be able to achieve just the amount of crazing you prefer.

While the ware is still quite hot from its final dousing with hot water, the ink is rubbed into the craze lines with a brush. The piece is then allowed to return to room temperature as the ink dries into the cracks. Finally, the excess ink is wiped off with damp paper towels or newspaper, and the permanently darkened crackle lines emerge in true, bold Ko style. One extra piece of advice: do *not* stain until you have the full crackle pattern you want. Piecemeal staining is rather too erratic in intensities; that is, the amount of stain absorbed by the craze lines varies from one time of application to another.

As an amusing (and, who knows, perhaps useful?) addendum to all this, we might consider the early eighteenth century Chinese technique for staining a ceramic piece, as reported by Père d'Entrecolles in one of his famous letters: "After it has been fired, it is boiled for some time in a very fat broth, and after that placed in the foulest sewer, where they leave it for a month or more."

A Note on Ju Ware

No book on Chinese celadons, especially Sung celadons, can afford to omit serious reference to Ju, that celebrated ware produced for a very brief period of time beginning in 1107 A.D., according to some authorities. The whole question of its provenance and characteristics is a vexed one, however. The first historic reference to it seems to have been made, for the purpose of comparison with Koryo, by a Chinese visitor to Korea, one Hsü Ching, in 1123. He remarks on the general resemblance of Koryo celadons to "Yüeh-chou and the new kiln wares of Ju-chou." Later references emphasize its rarity; and by the end of the century the general approach to Ju implies that it is a ware no longer made, one writer in 1192 stating that "Ju ware was made exclusively for the Palace. . . . Pieces rejected for use at the Palace were sold in the market, but they are very hard to obtain." In the West, today, authenticated Ju is so rare that the list compiled by Gompertz of known specimens outside of China and Taiwan contains only thirty-one pieces, of which fourteen are in the Percival David Collection in London, and three are in the United States. Even in the eighteenth century the Emperor Ch'ien Lung described Ju as "rare as the stars at dawn."

Exact identification of the color and texture of Ju ware, our main concern here, is apparently no simple matter. I do not intend to vex the question any more than it has been already, but in view of the possibility that Ju may really be related to some of the glazes in this book, I should mention some of the standard descriptions of it, despite their mutual contradictions. One ancient Chinese connoisseur calls Ju ware "sky blue," another, "ducks' egg color" (i.e., pale bluish or greenish), and adds that its texture is "transparent and thick like massed lard." Hobson has described the color as "precisely that of the most beautiful bluish green Corean bowls." Gompertz, it will be remembered from my section on Koryo, also remarked on the close resemblance between Korean celadons and both Ju *and* Lung-ch'üan. About Ju itself, he says: "The glaze is a smooth, opaque bluish green, often with a tinge of lavender . . . but there is some variation in the colour and in the type of crackle." And Garner further complicates things by describing a group of Ju specimens as having "a soft bluish-grey glaze of exquisite quality," and then going on to say of another Ju ware group that the glaze is "greenish rather than bluish." The final touch is added to the shifting picture by the same author's comment that a particular Chün piece with a "soft lavender glaze" would be hard to tell apart from Ju.

So what then *is* a typical Ju glaze? I dare not give an authoritative answer. But, frankly, I do have my suspicions. They are partly based on the five examples I was privileged to view during the exhibition of "Chinese Art Treasures" brought to this country from Taiwan in 1961. Four were crazed; one was not. The uncrazed one happened, in my opinion, to be the most beautiful of the lot. In the form of a "narcissus pot" or shallow oval dish with gently outward-sloping sides that rested on four simply carved feet, its light blue-green glaze and unblemished, slightly unctuous texture were pure perfection. The balance in the intensity of its colors was somehow just right; whereas some of the other Ju pieces, by comparison, seemed either too yellowish a green with insufficient blue, or too glossy and completely crazed, or a somewhat muddier mix of blue and green. I should add, however, that one of them was a delicate shallow bowl with a lovely light blue-green "ducks' egg" color. To cap this panorama of effects, the same exhibition contained another identically designed and dimensioned "narcissus pot" (exactly 23 cm. in length) with only slight differences in the shape of the carved feet; this one, however, also uncrazed, was a light *gray*-blue (or "sky blue"), and was described as Kuan ware!

My suspicions, then, are that a good number of the blue, lavender-tinged, blue-green, and gray-green glazes detailed in this and the preceding two chapters could be candidates, if one wished, for the "Ju" designation. It may seem presumptuous, but my suspicions are also partly based on the colors and textures of many of the pots I have made with these glazes. However hard one may work to stay within the confines of a particular celadon or Chün category, the delightful vagaries of the kiln often lead in other directions. So it is that certain of my glazes come to mind in this connection: the Chün and Kuan-Chün glazes, CIH-p, CIW-p, and CIZ-p are excellent possibilities, especially since the blues they create are often more assertive than the more grayed blues of much Chün and Kuan ware. (I am not referring here, of course, to those Chün pieces that are oversprayed with copper red.) The same is frequently true of my Koryo-type KCC#3, as well as SKA-F2. And at their bluest, my blue-green Kuan glazes, CEL#7, CEL#11, and CEL#14, are additional candidates.

As for the closely defined attributions sought by the connoisseurs, it would be well to recall one made by a very famous collector, that same Emperor Ch'ien Lung, whose enthusiastic poems about many of the pieces in his great collection are incised on their undersides. In the case of a particular lovely bowl, the special seal incised together with his poem refers to the glaze as "clear and unctuous"; the poem describes the bowl as a beautiful *"Chün."* Today's experts call this same piece a fine example of Ju.

In the naming of celadons, there would seem to be many options. But a lovely glaze by any other name. . . .

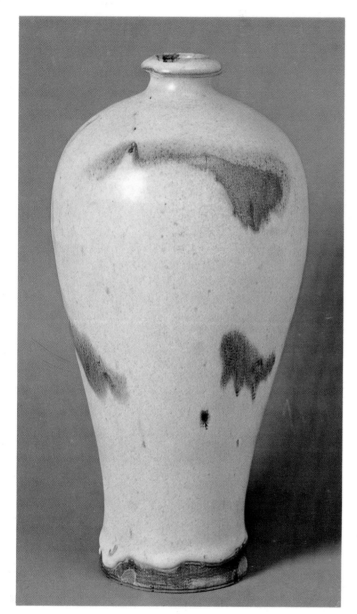

Chün. Large covered jar by the author. CIH-p glaze, dry milled. The iron blue is somewhat deeper than in most classic specimens. Note the less reduced area in the upper right portion.

Chün Ware. Mei P'ing vase. Late Sung or Yuan dynasties. 14″ x 6½″ (35.5 x 16.5 cm). Asian Art Museum of San Francisco. The Avery Brundage Collection. The thick blue glaze is typical of a reduced high-feldspathic composition containing wood ash and iron. The purple-red splashes are decorative applications of a reduced copper glaze.

Chün. Small section enlarged. CIH-p glaze, dry milled. Variegated dots range from blue and gray to green and brown and are interspersed with entrapped bubbles that fortify the overall blue.

Koryo Celadon. Ewer without cover. Koryo dynasty. 5¼″ x 7″ (13.3 x 17.7 cm). Asian Art Museum of San Francisco. The Avery Brundage Collection. Elegant simplicity of design and the perfection of the uncrazed glaze make this an outstanding specimen.

Koryo. Small bowl by the author. KCC#3 glaze. The blue-green is typical of this composition at its best when correctly milled and fully reduced.

Koryo. Small section enlarged. KCC#3 glaze. Thousands of tiny bubbles are closely massed together, contributing to the impression of blueness.

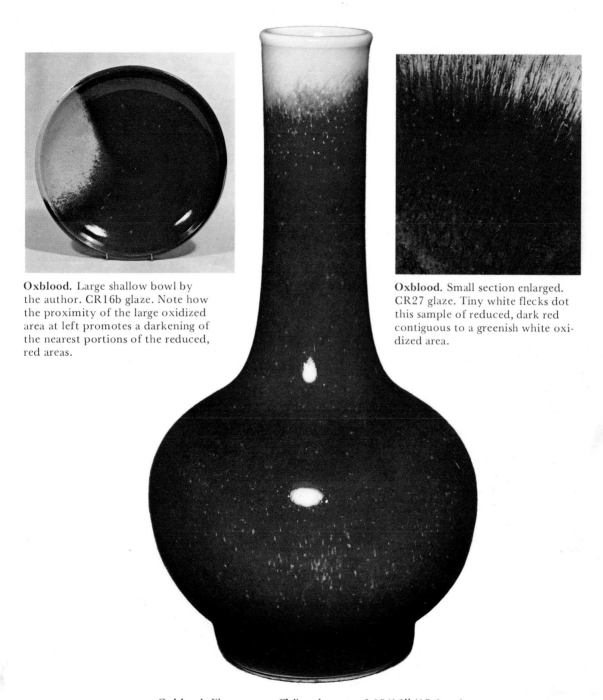

Oxblood. Large shallow bowl by
the author. CR16b glaze. Note how
the proximity of the large oxidized
area at left promotes a darkening of
the nearest portions of the reduced,
red areas.

Oxblood. Small section enlarged.
CR27 glaze. Tiny white flecks dot
this sample of reduced, dark red
contiguous to a greenish white oxidized area.

Oxblood. Flower vase. Ch'ing dynasty. 6 15/16" (17.6 cm)
high. Courtesy of the Smithsonian Institution, Freer Gallery
of Art, Washington, D.C. The color exemplifies the right
balance between reduction and oxidation of the copper
red glaze. The white flecks and the pale greenish white
around the upper neck further demonstrate this fact.

Chien Oil Spot. Tea bowl. Sung dynasty. 7 5/8″ (19.4 cm) diameter. Courtesy of the Smithsonian Institution, Freer Gallery of Art, Washington, D.C. The large size and clear pattern of its silvery iridescent spots, as well as its ample diameter for a tea bowl, make this an unusual piece.

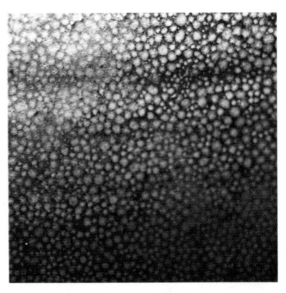

Oil Spot. Small bowl by the author. T+C6 glaze. The small, iridescent spots are actually iron-rich crystals that are closely distributed over the entire surface of the glaze.

Oil Spot. Small section enlarged. T+C6 glaze. Each spot exhibits a grayish, radiating crystal pattern.

Lung-ch'üan Ware. (Kinuta type.) Mallet-shaped vase with phoenix handles. Sung dynasty. 11″ (27.9 cm) high. Reproduced by permission of the Syndics of the Fitzwilliam Museum, Cambridge. The smooth, soft texture and delicately balanced blue-green color of this piece ideally represent the "kinuta" quality.

Lung-ch'üan Type. Ovate vase by the author. EP#4 glaze. The glaze is a deep sea green with a hint of blue, but is more translucent and less unctuous than the superb specimen at left.

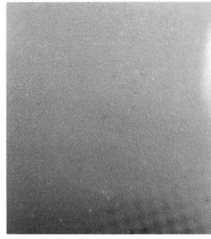

Lung-ch'üan Type. Small section enlarged. ACG8 glaze. The countless, close-packed bubbles heighten the suggestion of blue in this essentially gray-green glaze and also promote an increase in unctuosity over EP#4.

Northern Celadon. Saucer dish with carved chrysanthemum design. Sung dynasty. 8 1/8″ (20.6 cm) diameter. Reproduced by permission of the Syndics of the Fitzwilliam Museum, Cambridge. The three-dimensionality of the design is heightened by the pooling of the glaze.

Northern Celadon Type. Small vase and bottles by the author. KCC#6 glaze on the two at left; ACGW-FK6 glaze on one at right.

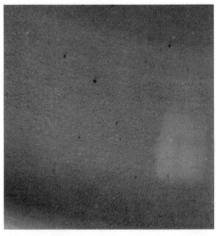

Northern Celadon Type. Small section enlarged. ACG7-F3 glaze. The structure of the glaze is basically close-grained.

Kuan Ware. Bottle. Sung dynasty. 6¼″ (15.8 cm) high. Courtesy of the Percival David Foundation of Chinese Art, University of London. The soft, semi-matte texture and the pale gray color permeated by a delicate suggestion of blue make this an excellent representative of one variety of Kuan.

Kuan Type. Two bowls by the author. CIZ-p2 glaze at left; CEL#16 glaze at right. The soft whitish gray matte of CIZ-p2 has a blue cast; CEL#16 tends more to greenish gray tones.

Kuan Type. Small section enlarged. CIZ-p2 glaze. Note the "worm-track" markings.

Kuan Ware. (Ko type.) Foliate bowl. Sung dynasty. 7 11/16″ (19.6 cm) diameter. Courtesy of the Percival David Foundation of Chinese Art, University of London. This is an outstanding example of the typical Ko style with its gray glaze strongly marked by wide-spaced, dark brown crackle suggestive of the "crab's claw" pattern.

Ko Type. Broad-based bowl and small conical bowl by the author. KCC#3 glaze at left; SKA glaze at right. Both exhibit the large-spaced "crab's claw" crackle pattern. In color and texture, KCC#3 is closer to Koryo; SKA, to Kuan.

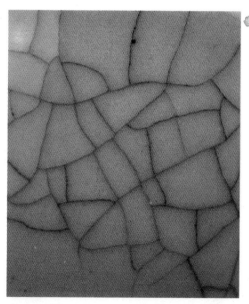

Ko Type. Small section enlarged. SKA glaze.

Ju Ware. Bowl. Sung dynasty. 6 5/8″ (16.8 cm) diameter. Courtesy of the Percival David Foundation of Chinese Art, University of London. This fine specimen, with its pale blue suffusion of the crackled, Kuan-like matte glaze, demonstrates how closely one provenance verges on another. This is the bowl that the Emperor Ch'ien Lung described as a choice example of Chün.

Ju Type. Bowl and vase by the author. CIZ-p at left; CIW-p at right. The franker, bolder statement of blue resembles that found in the remarkable Ju vase belonging to the Mrs. Alfred Clark collection (pictured in Gompertz and Swann).

Ju Type. Small section enlarged. CIW-p glaze. Though noticeably finer textured and lighter colored, this is quite similar in structure to that of Chün.

Peach Bloom. Water pot. Ch'ing dynasty. 2 3/4" x 5" (7 x 12.7 cm) Victoria and Albert Museum, Crown Copyright. This is the most beautiful example of the peach bloom glaze that has ever come to my attention. The isolated and massed dots of deep red seem to float in a soft matrix of rich pink with a suggestion of purple.

Peach Bloom. Large bowl by the author. Aged CR16b glaze. Though more translucent than the Chinese prototype, it shows the pattern of dots.

Peach Bloom Small section enlarged. Aged CR16b glaze. The dark red "dots" appear here as copper-rich clumpings scattered through the pink areas.

Chien Hare's Fur. Tea bowl. Sung dynasty. 2½″ (6.4 cm) high. Courtesy of the Ashmolean Museum, Oxford. The light-colored streaks are formed by crystalline spots of iron pulled into rough columns by the flow of the surrounding, darker glaze matrix. Viewed at a slight distance, the overall effect resembles the markings of animal fur.

Hare's Fur Type. Bottle by the author. T#15 glaze. The light-colored streaks are narrower than in most classic specimens.

Hare's Fur Type. Small section enlarged. T#14Co glaze. The darker lines of flow are interspersed with columns of yellowish iron-rich crystals.

Tz'u-chou Ware. Vase with painted decorations. Sung dynasty. 9 5/16″ (23.6 cm) high. Courtesy of the Trustees of the British Museum. The perfectly balanced, generous form and the bold yet sensitive brushwork combine to make a masterpiece. Note the soft-textured effect achieved by the white slip and the thin, clear glaze over it.

Tz'u-chou Type. Shallow bowl by the author. ACGW-H4 glaze over white slip. The underglaze decoration is sharply defined under the clear glaze. which blends into a semi-matte with the white slip.

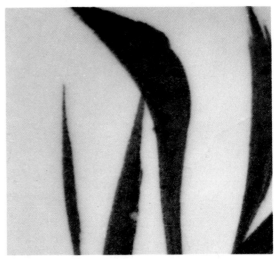

Tz'u-chou Type. Small section enlarged. ACGW-H4 glaze over white slip, The brushstroke outlines retain their sharpness under the glaze.

Blue-spotted Glaze: KCC+Y2. Vase by the author. This unusual glaze is the one I had lost for eight years. It has no classic or modern prototypes.

Turquoise. Bowls, vase, and tile by the author. AT#18 glaze. The variations in brilliancy and softness are conditioned by thickness of application and by firing conditions. Some Tz'u-chou brush-decorated ware is glazed with clear turquoise.

Yao Pien Temmoku Type. Bottle and shallow bowl by the author. The basic glaze is T#14Co with "spots" excavated and replaced with CIH-p.

Dark Blue-and-Brown Mottled. Large bottle by the author. C+GA1F1 glaze. The full range of clumped colors from light and dark blue to brown requires an exact balancing of reduction and oxidation.

Kuan-Chün. Pieces by the author. The following wet-milled glazes were used as indicated: CIW-p for the vase and the covered jar; CIZ-p for the smaller bowl; CIH-m for the larger bowl; and CIW-p2 for the flat-rimmed dish.

Spotted Kuan-Chün. Bowl and three vases by the author. CIH-m glaze dry milled. The brown specks which are distributed irregularly through the stony matte surface are apparently iron-rich clumps.

Combined Glazes. Pieces by the author. For the pitcher, both T#14Co and wet-milled CIH-p were used. For the other three pieces, KCC+Y2 was the basic glaze, with areas reserved by means of two separate paper resists for wet-milled CIH-p and T#14Co.

Combined Glazes. Three large vases by the author. At left and right, CIH-p is used side-by-side with T#14Co. The center vase employs CIH-p under T#14Co, except in limited areas reserved by paper resists for T#14Co alone.

4
DARK
BLUE-AND-BROWN
MOTTLED IRON
GLAZES

We now turn our attention to a pair of glazes of some distinction which, to my knowledge, have neither modern counterparts nor classic antecedents. They are simply fine glazes that have evolved out of my experimentation with some of the same materials utilized in various compositions already described in these pages. As will be seen, both glazes employ granite powder and softwood ash. The special adjustments in proportion, however, produce glazes of distinctly new and different finish, surface, and aesthetic appeal.

The most desirable coloration, in my opinion, for these types is a variegation on the surface of the finished pot that has passages of matte-textured mottling in tiny, irregular specks and splashes of bright blue and rich brown. These passages run into others of very vivid dark blue that in turn are sharply demarcated (by the fluid lines of kiln atmosphere movement) from yet other passages possessing more muted, slightly over-reduced colors, or conversely, rich, partly oxidized browns. In effect, then, the one pot produces effects of oxidation, reduction-with-oxidation, and heavy reduction, all running into and abutting on each other in subtle, natural gradations. (To achieve these and similar results, the reader should follow the special directions for firing detailed at the end of this chapter.)

Occasionally the work-heat in the kiln is so intensely effective that a greater fluidity occurs and no matte surfaces appear. When this quality is balanced with just the right degree of reduction-with-oxidation to produce a more vivid blue, the total appearance of the finished glaze is most striking and sumptuous. The recommended type of ware body to be used with these two glazes is a buff stoneware that fires in reduction to a soft gray color.

C+GA1F1

The first of the two glazes exhibits a larger-speckled mottling than does the second, with a bolder, more vivid effect and a greater tendency to extremes of variegation on the one pot.

Batch Recipe	Buckingham feldspar	26.5
	Granite powder	21.5
	Whiting	17.0
	Georgia kaolin	3.5
	Flint	23.5
	Softwood ash	8.0
		100.0
	Red iron oxide (3% of batch)	3.0

Dunting versus Crazing. It is interesting to observe how slight is the apparent difference in composition between this and the following glaze. The most striking distinctions occur in the relative proportions of feldspar to flint. The harder surface of the C1+G6F1 glaze is probably attributable to the eutectic achieved by its special balancing of these two components. At the same time, there is a consequent tendency of this glaze to cause dunting or shivering on certain stoneware bodies; and, conversely, C+GA1F1 has an equally inherent tendency to craze on certain other clay bodies. A proper matching of body to glaze in each case prevents both these tendencies. See Chapter 11 and *Glossary* for more specific information on this point.

C1+G6F1

The other glaze of distinction in this particular group usually presents an appearance of subtler refinement and greater finish. The specks of color (blue, brown, etc.) are smaller grained and more regular in size and shape, the surface is smoother, and the overall texture exhibits a more uniform "melt." Whereas the first glaze usually makes its appeal more boldly and ruggedly, this one does so quietly and delicately.

Batch Recipe	Buckingham feldspar	20.85
	Granite powder	21.55
	Whiting	16.42
	Georgia kaolin	3.36
	Flint	29.52
	Softwood ash	8.3
		100.00
	Red iron oxide (3% of batch)	3.0

Procedures for C+GA1F1 and C1+G6F1. Follow the directions for mixing, applying, and drying given in Chapter 1. *Dry*-mill for about one hour. Application to the ware should be fairly thick.

Both these glazes do best when fired to cone 10, but in an only *moderately* heavy reduction firing. In other words, the amount of blue flame visible at the stack in the latter stages of the firing should be *lessened* enough to produce a more delicate balance between reduction and oxidation. If the glaze is overreduced, its color will become somewhat muted and muddy; if overoxidized, it will run to a deep, though not unattractive brown. (An analogous situation in the firing of copper red glazes will be found in Chapter 5.) Although the same basic steps in firing given in Chapter 1 should be adhered to, these important exceptions must be made in the following steps:

3. Terminate this step somewhat earlier, at about 1425°F. (774°C.), at which point moderate reduction should be initiated.

5. The fuller degree of reduction should be started at 1650°F. (899°C.).

6. At 1875°F. (1024°C.), the fullest possible reduction should be contrived, as in the case of Chün, for three-quarters of an hour.

8. Especially toward the final hour, the gas, air, and flue openings should be arranged to achieve the *lightest* possible quality of blue flame at the stack, so that only the faintest degree of reduction is maintained in the kiln. In other words, the state of atmosphere should be a bit more in the direction of reduction than what is sometimes described as "neutral."

5
COPPER RED
AND
PEACH BLOOM

A copper red glaze of fine quality is one of the most elusive to achieve and difficult to repeat with consistency. Its color ranges from a vibrant, dark blood-red to the lightest suffusions of pink. The former are often called "oxblood," *sang-de-boeuf*, or *lang yao*; the latter are usually referred to as "peach bloom." In some cases, the red may be purplish; in others, it may be touched with hints or streaks of milky blue, the resulting alternations of red and blue making up what is known as *flambé*.

Oxblood

The oxblood glaze itself is often variegated (mainly because of kiln conditions), with oxidized greenish or bluish areas adjacent to those of the darkest red; frequently, it is also marked with small splotches of deeper or lighter red in certain sections. Another common characteristic is the tendency to develop crazing in the oxidized areas. The texture of an oxblood glaze is usually glassy, with a multitude of tiny, unbroken bubbles remaining in the matrix, but also revealing minute pitmarks where some of these bubbles have broken and then healed at the glaze surface.

The earliest overall copper red pots of record go back to Hsüan-tê in the Ming dynasty, and the great era of Chinese oxblood glaze production was later reached in the K'ang Hsi period of the Ch'ing. Even earlier than these, however are the numerous Chün pots of the Sung dynasty which are decorated with splashes and blushes of copper red, sometimes suffusing the whole surface of the glaze. Apparently, the technique of gaining red coloration via reduced copper was well within the grasp of the Sung potter, despite his limited use of it.

I am aware that this group of glazes has been much discussed and fully investigated by researchers, and sometimes by potters, in many places and at many times; and I not only have read many articles and studies on the matter, but also have seen contemporary pots that are glazed in some form of copper red. In general, though, there seems to have been more talk than performance; and when that talk was sometimes fashionably belittling of oxbloods, as I have on occasion noticed, there was no performance at all. My general impression, then, is that the art-potter frequently lacks the necessary technical information to produce what is unquestionably a beautiful variety of glaze. It is therefore my hope that the material contained in this chapter may help other interested potters achieve satisfactory results with copper reds more easily and effectively.

Oxblood Glaze Formulas and Recipes

Fundamental to the empirical formulas and batch recipes detailed below is the addition of only just the right amounts of copper. It will be noted how extremely small these amounts are, never reaching even four-tenths of one percent of the total batch weight. The use of more than one-half of one percent of copper oxide would be most inadvisable, since it would only tend to muddy the color of the fired glaze. Another basic characteristic of these glaze compositions is the presence of tin oxide to the amount of roughly three to five times the quantity of the copper. During reduction firing, the tin oxide's function is to help scatter and stabilize those particles of colloidal copper that comprise the relatively wide red layer in the glaze. (The physical structure of the glaze in layers is explained later in this chapter.)

The first three glazes here should be fired to no more than cone 9; the fourth one can go as high as cone 10 for the effects indicated. The firing procedures for all four should follow the special, basic patterns given later in this chapter.

CR 16b

This is probably the best of my oxbloods in most respects.

Empirical Formula	$.2493\ Na_2O$	$.45926\ Al_2O_3$	$3.324\ SiO_2$
	$.1385\ K_2O$	$.34626\ B_2O_3$	
	$.6121\ CaO$		

Batch Recipe	Nepheline syenite	166.32
	Buckingham feldspar	35.76
	Georgia kaolin	7.74
	Flint	88.74
	Colemanite	51.5
	Whiting	41.3
		391.36
	Copper oxide (0.3% of batch)	1.17
	Tin oxide (1.0% of batch)	3.91

CR 27

This glaze vies with the preceding one in producing the richest, darkest reds when fired correctly.

Empirical Formula	$.3125\ Na_2O$	$.4625\ Al_2O_3$	$3.2093\ SiO_2$
	$.1041\ K_2O$	$.3139\ B_2O_3$	
	$.5832\ CaO$		

Batch Recipe	Nepheline syenite	206.97
	Colemanite	46.35
	Whiting	40.20
	Flint	82.20
		375.72
	Copper oxide (0.385% of batch)	1.45
	Tin oxide (1.0% of batch)	3.75

CR 28a

This dark red glaze, though very beautiful at its best, is particularly sensitive to the muddying influences of overreduction; also, because of its soda ash content, it requires special care in avoiding excessive water when preparing it for application. Attention should be paid to the procedural explanations given later on handling these problems.

Empirical Formula .4651 Na_2O .4625 Al_2O_3 3.2093 SiO_2
.1041 K_2O .3139 B_2O_3
.4306 CaO

Batch Recipe	Nepheline syenite	206.976
	Soda ash	17.384
	Colemanite	46.35
	Whiting	23.80
	Flint	82.20
		376.71
	Copper oxide (0.2% of batch)	.75
	Tin oxide (1.0% of batch)	3.76

CR 17

The fourth and last formulation I give here for oxbloods might be considered transitional to the peach bloom glazes presented later in this chapter. When fired to cone 10, it becomes a deep, semi-matte red; when fired to cone 9, it produces a peach bloom of somewhat more matte surface. Occasionally, where it runs thick, it develops a slight bluish opalescence. It is also exceptional in that it seems to resist crystallization when stored wet, and so it can be used without being made fresh each time.

Empirical Formula .2503 Na_2O .4593 Al_2O_3 3.4404 SiO_2
.1406 K_2O .2812 B_2O_3
.6090 CaO

Batch Recipe	Godfrey (or Maine) feldspar	301.07
	Colemanite	41.2
	Whiting	45.0
		387.27
	Copper oxide (0.3% of batch)	1.16
	Tin oxide (1.0% of batch)	3.87

Opalescence in Copper Red Glazes

The phenomenon of opalescence in a copper red glaze (for example, in CR 17 above) is largely owing to an excess of silica in relation to a given amount of alumina in the glaze composition. Thus, for *flambé* effects, extra increments of silica will generally produce streaks or flecks of bluish opalescence and at the same time intensify the clarity of the crimson portions. Conversely, extra increments of alumina will both eliminate all signs of opalescence and push the red towards a dull scarlet rather than a brilliant crimson. If the goal is a true oxblood, an exact balance must be maintained between the alumina and the silica. So delicate is this balance, I should add, that even the natural mineral content of the water used for the glaze mix may upset it by containing excessive quantities of either alumina or silica. (In this regard, note the experiment conducted with water in the making of copper turquoise glazes in Chapter 6.)

Procedure for Oxblood and Peach Bloom Glazes. See basic directions in Chapter 1 for mixing the glaze ingredients. All the glazes in the general category of oxbloods and peach blooms must be thoroughly milled. However, since most of them do not keep well in the wet state, and after a time crystallize in part, it is best to *dry*-mill them first. Thus, one can store dry glaze in jars indefinitely and can convert to the wet condition only so much glaze as is needed for applying to the pots planned for a particular firing. Of course, if a more even-colored effect is desired, the glaze can be re-milled wet. For most purposes, though, I find this last step unnecessary. In either case, freshly made-up glaze applied promptly will yield the best colors.

In applying the glaze follow most carefully the basic directions given in Chapter 1. The only exception is the omission of corn syrup from the glaze mix, as this substance tends to overthin these particular glazes and to make them flake more uncontrollably in large patches. For the rest, extra-special caution in following the application procedures should be maintained. For example, when adding water to the dry glaze, do so *very* gradually so as to avoid thinning out the mixture too much and, hence, overwetting the ware in application. Overthinning or applying the glaze in too thick a coat will almost certainly produce hairline cracking, crawling, or peeling not long after the glaze is applied. The fired result will be a pot disfigured by bare spots and thick running streaks, often down past the foot onto the shelves, caused by the lifting up and folding back of the glaze on itself during the firing.

One last piece of advice here: considering the very fluid nature of most of these particular glazes, the potter would be very wise to leave *unglazed* an area of about 1" or so up from the foot on each pot. (A full account of how to reserve such an unglazed area when using a spray gun is given in Chapter 7 under "Procedures for Hare's Fur and Partridge Feather Glazes.") Such an area will allow for some running of the glaze, but without the possibility of its reaching the foot of the pot and the shelf beneath it.

Follow the directions in Chapter 1 for drying the glaze. No less than one week should be given this process. If the glaze is fired before it is bone dry, it will certainly crawl and peel from the ware in large unsightly patches.

Use of White Slip under Copper Red Glazes

I have often achieved especially brilliant reds by applying the glaze to a buff body already bisqued with a coating of white slip. Best results are obtained when the slip is *first* applied to the leatherhard greenware and then bisqued with it. White slip *later* applied to ware that has already been bisqued frequently causes raised, whitened bumps under the surface of the fired red glaze, owing to poor adherence of the slip. For the smoothest, most even coating of white slip, I usually thin it out a bit with one or two teaspoons of corn syrup and then apply it to the ware with a spray gun. Brushing the slip on will yield less satisfactory results for this purpose. See Chapter 11 for the white slip recipes I most often use.

Peach Bloom

Peach bloom is a comparatively rare, very delicate, appealing glaze. It is characterized by a prevailing soft pink color in which are interspersed both spots and passages of deeper red. In some cases, a few of the scattered spots are green; at times there is also the faintest suggestion of purple in the pink matrix.

Peach Bloom Glaze Formulas and Recipes

The same proportions and functions of copper oxide and tin oxide already noted above under the oxblood recipes are equally true for peach bloom glazes. That is, the percentage of copper in each batch recipe is again well under four-tenths of one percent, and the added tin oxide likewise approximates three times the quantity of the copper oxide. The paler colors produced in peach bloom glazes are related to other factors than these two.

CR 18

The first glaze in this group follows numerically and logically after the final one described under oxbloods. CR18 is a good peach bloom, though probably not my best, similar in composition to CR 17, but lighter in color and more matte in texture. Like CR 17, when fired to cone 10 it approaches oxblood; at cone 9 it merits its lighter peach bloom description. Unlike CR 17, it almost never develops opalescence.

Empirical Formula	$.2542\ Na_2O$	$.4666\ Al_2O_3$	$3.4952\ SiO_2$
	$.1428\ K_2O$	$.2142\ B_2O_3$	
	$.6028\ CaO$		

Batch Recipe	Godfrey (or Maine) feldspar	301.07
	Colemanite	30.9
	Whiting	48.3
		380.27
	Copper oxide (0.3% of batch)	1.14
	Tin oxide (1.0% of batch)	3.8

CR 25Z1

This is one of the finest and most delicate peach blooms, especially when not applied too thickly. It is to be fired to cone 9.

Empirical Formula	.2511 Na$_2$O	.4626 Al$_2$O$_3$	3.2093 SiO$_2$
	.1395 K$_2$O	.3139 B$_2$O$_3$	
	.5441 CaO		
	.0651 ZnO		

Batch Recipe	Nepheline syenite	166.32
	Buckingham feldspar	35.76
	Georgia kaolin	7.74
	Flint	79.74
	Colemanite	46.35
	Whiting	36.00
	Zinc oxide	5.67
		377.58
	Copper oxide (0.385% of batch)	1.45
	Tin oxide (1.0% of batch)	3.77

CR 26

Here we have a rather unusual variety of copper red glaze that might be classified as a peach bloom for want of any other established category. In composition, it is actually midway between CR 17 and CR 18; however, in color (probably because of the faint, almost indiscernible suggestion of opalescent blue) it is a rather deep rose red with a semi-matte texture.

Empirical Formula	.2528 Na$_2$O	.4640 Al$_2$O$_3$	3.4753 SiO$_2$
	.1420 K$_2$O	.2414 B$_2$O$_3$	
	.6051 CaO		

Batch Recipe	Godfrey (or Maine) feldspar	301.07
	Colemanite	35.02
	Whiting	46.97
		383.06
	Copper oxide (0.385% of batch)	1.47
	Tin oxide (1.0% of batch)	3.83

Aged CR 16b

For this final entry on my peach bloom glazes, I have reserved what is certainly the best, probably the most authentic, of them all, and at the same time the most difficult one to achieve consistently. Personally, I am convinced that the simple but troublesome technique I have developed for this glaze is probably the same as that once used by the K'ang Hsi potters, though I have found no reference to this idea in any of the literature. I base this conclusion on the following facts: (1) my glaze, when successful, is often identical in appearance with one class of K'ang Hsi peach blooms; (2) the number of K'ang Hsi peach blooms still in existence is far outnumbered by oxbloods; (3) the latter fact is logically related to the difficulty of controlling this glaze at all times; (4) the equally logical and natural fact that the K'ang Hsi potters could easily have come by this glaze in the same fashion as I did is most obvious. If all this sounds portentous, let me dispel this impression at once by straightforward explanation.

My much-valued peach bloom, then, is nothing but my CR 16b (detailed first in the oxblood section above) made up *wet*, stored for a time so as to *encourage* partial decomposition and crystallization, and *then* applied to the ware. The difficulties that arise in this procedure are basically twofold: (1) The glaze must not be *too* old, or it will "spit out" during the firing — indeed, all over the kiln furniture — and will crawl badly on the ware. (2) The crystallization of the wet glaze makes it very difficult to apply, especially when one uses a spray gun, in which case it tends to clog the gun.

But it is these very difficulties, or rather the qualities implicit in their causes, that make possible the special beauty of this glaze. The clumping of particles in tiny specks, when the glaze is applied to the ware, later yields intensely rich, dark red spots (and, typically, occasional green spots) in the fired results. Also, the decomposition of the rest of the wet glaze, producing a kind of separation of soft from hard (crystalline) substances, creates the basic overall quality of the fired glaze: a soft, delicate, pinkish color of great depth. The combined effect is that of dark red specks floating in a rich matrix of subtle pink. It is well worth the difficulties involved.

Firing Procedures for Oxblood and Peach Bloom Glazes. Besides proper composition and most careful application, copper reds require firing conditions that must be regulated and controlled with special care. Although these glazes are of the reduction variety, there are degrees to everything, and in this case the balance between reduction and oxidation must be engineered even more carefully than in those of Chün, Kuan, Lung-ch'üan, and the others I have previously described. For example, if there is too much reduction, an oxblood glaze will become a muddy, brownish red that is hardly attractive; if there is too much oxidation, it will bleach out to an almost completely colorless, or sometimes faintly greenish, hue. The same glaze fired so as to avoid either of these extremes often becomes a vividly brilliant, deep red.

It is also noteworthy and significant that many copper red pots may be variegated in broad, separate areas, owing to the pattern of currents of both reduction and oxidation atmospheres within the kiln. On such pots, the intensity of the color follows a quite definable form: those surfaces that are directly contiguous to areas that have been overoxidized and hence bleached white are *always* the deepest, darkest reds or the richest pinks; conversely, those surfaces that are farthest removed from the oxidized portions run to quieter, more muted pinks. The basic significance of this phenomenon, I believe, is the fact that *just* the right amount of oxidation applied to the reduced glaze yields the best, richest, freshest reds and pinks. In fact, it accomplishes this result all over a nonvariegated pot when it receives the best balance of these two opposing atmospheres.

Another important consideration in firing oxbloods and peach blooms is the temperature range, which must be carefully limited. The glazes I have detailed in this chapter should be fired, in most cases, to no more than cone 9. At cone 10, their copper tends either to volatilize completely or to fade to dullish pink, instead of deep red or the true, soft pink of a peach bloom.

With the foregoing comments in mind, then, let me point up the essential differences in firing procedures from those described in Chapter 1. All the stages outlined there should be followed, *but with these important exceptions in the following steps:*

3. Terminate this step somewhat earlier, at about 1425°F. (774°C.), at which point moderate reduction should be initiated.

5. The fuller degree of reduction should be started at 1650°F. (899°C.).

6. At 1875°F. (1024°C.) the fullest possible reduction should be contrived, as in the case of Chün, for three-quarters of an hour.

8. Especially toward the final hour, arrange gas, air, and flue openings to achieve the *lightest* possible quality of blue flame at the stack, so that only the faintest degree of reduction is maintained within the kiln. In other words, the state of atmosphere should be a bit more in the direction of reduction than what is sometimes described as "neutral."

9. Carry the firing only to cone 9; when this cone is bent flat, the firing should be stopped. Except where indicated for certain effects in glazes CR 17 and CR 18, as described above, it would be quite inadvisable to carry the firing beyond this cone.

The Physical Structure of Fired Oxblood Glaze

It should be of interest and invaluable, practical assistance to the serious potter to understand not only the outward appearance of a fired oxblood glaze, but also its physical structure. Such understanding should better enable the potter to grapple with the special challenges involved in making this glaze. Fortunately, this structure has been ably analyzed and microphotographed by B. Moore and J.W. Mellor and interestingly reported by A.L. Hetherington (see *Bibliography*).

I shall present their complex analysis here, reduced to its barest facts. When fired in a reduction atmosphere, the copper in an oxblood glaze becomes finely divided into several different particle sizes, some of it even achieving a colloidal state. The reducing agents, tin oxide and iron oxide, are also of great assistance in producing this result. The final fired glaze, when studied in cross-section by microphotograph, reveals not one, but *five* layers of color. The stratum contiguous to the body is *colorless* or *gray*; next to this layer is a thin one of *blue*; just above the blue is a third, much broader band of *red*; then above the red lies a thin layer of *yellow* (though occasionally this is missing); finally, at the outer surface of the glaze is a fairly broad, fifth area of *colorless* or *faintly greenish* glaze.

The explanation of this range of color from the *one* oxide (copper oxide) has to do with the relative size of the separate particles of copper. Total solution of the copper in the glaze renders it colorless, as in the lowest layer; extremely fine particles still floating in the glaze give the visual impression of yellow; slightly larger particles render that portion of the glaze red; and still larger particles of copper produce the blue layer. The faintly greenish layer at the top is owing to the re-oxidation of the surface of the glaze during the latter stage of the firing. (Oxidized copper normally turns green.)

In all of this, the role of oxygen as it works on a reduced glaze is prime. The entire process of developing the various particle sizes, and thus the different color layers, is dependent on the effect of aerial oxygen working its way down into the already reduced glaze: the more vigorous its action, as at the outset of its influence, the smaller the copper particle size; the less vigorous its effect, the larger the particle size.

Hence the progression of smaller particle color (yellow) to largest particle color (blue). With the blue layer, all the effect of the aerial oxygen is consumed; thus it never reaches or affects the colorless, reduced layer next to the body of the ware itself. Of course, the remarkable thing in all this is the net optical effect of this complex color structure: the one color, red.

The Physical Structure of Fired Peach Bloom Glaze

As might be gathered from the uneven, patchy distributions of color in a peach bloom glaze, its physical structure does not consistently conform to the five-layer pattern of color typical of the oxblood glaze, as described in the preceding section. Clearly, the copper oxide in the peach bloom is so irregularly distributed that in some areas of a piece it is rendered pink by the action of the aerial oxygen, and in others, where it is more concentrated or even clumped, it is turned into deep red. In the pink areas, the normal red layer is not nearly so broad as it is in the oxblood glaze, and thus the optical effect of redness is diminished; in some cases, the red even merges into a purplish or bluish pink tinge because of the blue layer below it. In yet other areas on certain specimens, the pink grades off into a yellowish tinge; here there is no band of red in the glaze structure at all. On the other hand, the red spots elsewhere contain a sufficiency of copper oxide to build up, under the impact of the aerial oxygen, a significant layer of red.

The occasional green spots are another matter. These are probably formed by the oxidation, again via aerial oxygen, of colloidal clumpings of copper oxide in the glaze which are so concentrated that they fill most of the physical structure of the glaze in vertical section from top to bottom. Hence, these dots become fully oxidized, and therefore green, under the attack of the oxygen in the last stages of the firing.

All the above characteristics, incidentally, are to be found in the fired results of the fifth peach bloom glaze described above, Aged CR 16b.

Local Reduction Oxblood Glazes

Before closing this chapter, something should be added concerning "local reduction" copper reds. The simple addition of very finely divided (600 mesh or more) *silicon carbide* powder to such glazes as CR 16b or CR 27 will produce very interesting results. A proportion of about 0.3% of silicon carbide is just about right for this purpose.

Local Reduction Firing Procedures and Results

The firing itself must be very carefully controlled. First of all, the kiln must be set, from start to finish, for a purely *oxidizing* atmosphere. In other words, one must rigidly avoid smoke, back pressure at the peepholes, flame at the stack, etc. Second, the ware must not be fired any higher than cones 7 or 7-plus. There are at least two reasons for this latter consideration: (1) the addition of the silicon carbide makes these glazes even more runny than they normally are in a regular reduction firing; (2) the local reduction "atmosphere," in an otherwise *oxidation* firing is indeed quite "local" to the pots glazed for it, and is therefore a relatively temporary phenomenon.

This last point means that, above a certain temperature, the reducing efficiency of the carbon in the silicon carbide will gradually diminish to zero. Thus, there will be little or no red color left in an overfired glaze, or at best some few streaks of red running down to a pool in the center of a bowl. This characteristic points up one of the less desirable possibilities in a local reduction copper red: it has a definite tendency to mottlings against a buff or white background. (Incidentally, for the latter quality white slip is again especially desirable as a background for local reduction reds; it is more attractive than the oxidized buff hue of the unslipped clay.) However, if the glaze application and the firing are carefully regulated, a very beautiful rich red can be produced on many pieces. Indeed, one sure advantage of this type of copper red is that the color itself, in whatever pattern it may appear, is consistently dark and glowing.

This last fact underscores my earlier observation about the richest, freshest reds being found in the closest physical proximity to the completely oxidized areas on a piece fired with normal reduction methods. Obviously, the constant availability of a supply of *oxygen* in an *oxidation* firing of local reduction reds yields this *overall* freshness of color for the latter type. All of which adds up to further confirmation of what we already know: the fact that reduction *and* oxidation are both necessary to the creation of the best copper reds. In the case of this particular phenomenon, the chemicophysical explanations still await scientific elucidation over and above the light already thrown on the subject by Moore, Mellor, and Hetherington (see *Bibliography*).

A word about kilns in this regard. An electric kiln is probably more reliable for handling local reduction reds than is a gas kiln; at least, that has been my experience. A gas kiln often tends to create *some* reduction, even when it is not wanted.

And a final caution for experimenters who may wish to try silicon carbide with other glazes. In my experience, it does not work well with other than glossy, fluid ones. The resistance offered to the release of the carbon in those mixtures that are more or less viscous creates unsightly craters in the glaze which do not plane out, or, where they do, leave unattractive blotches.

6
TURQUOISE

Despite its more usual Persian provenance as a low-fired earthenware, turquoise in its high-fired forms is an authentic, if somewhat rare, late Sung glaze. It is to be found on certain of the handsomely brush-decorated stonewares of Tz'u-chou where it substitutes for the more usual covering of clear, colorless glaze. Quite unlike the darker, staring cobalt blues of the later Ming and, especially, Ch'ing glazes, copper turquoise has a subtler, more delicate, and yet more brilliant quality; typically, the glaze itself is always finely crazed. The turquoise color can be achieved only in a highly alkaline glaze of a particular type, which, incidentally, is the reason for the inevitable crazing. The special challenge of a *high-fired* turquoise on semi-vitreous stoneware, as distinguished from the lovely, but porous Persian earthenware, presents additional problems. But it is a challenge that evidently can be met successfully, if only because it has so been met before.

Special Problems in Formulation

The basic problem is the sensitivity of the turquoise color to the presence of alumina in the glaze. The slightest amount of alumina in excess of the permissible maximum will completely destroy the essential blue quality. Thus, the chief difficulty in composing the ideal turquoise glaze is to keep it as free as possible of alumina and yet to supply it with enough alkali to offset the tendency of the latter to volatilize along with the copper at relatively high temperatures. As a result, the glaze is somewhat difficult to handle, since such stabilizing influences as kaolin simply cannot be included in the formulation.

Another important limitation is the fact that the choice of alkali is not an open question. Calcium or magnesia must be excluded because they encourage green hues at the expense of the desired blue. Thus, we are more or less limited to potassium oxide or sodium oxide. Here, too, as I have found from experience, one is better than the other, sodium being definitely preferable to potassium for the turquoise color. But this fact, in turn, compounds the difficulties. For one is forced, in calculating a glaze with such special requirements, to introduce sodium in the form of raw soda ash, a substance whose solubility renders this "prima donna" glaze even more elusive and unpredictable.

All these limitations and restrictions in the formulation, as well as in the handling, of this type of glaze perhaps explain its comparative rarity. Certainly one possible reason for the emergence in later Chinese ceramics of cobalt, with its strong, dark hues, as the dominant blue colorant is to be found in its relative ease of handling as compared with the special difficulties surrounding the use of copper for turquoise at high temperatures.

By now it is obvious that extra precautions must be taken all along the line to insure good results with stoneware turquoise glazes. Careful attention must therefore be paid to all of the procedural advice given in this chapter.

AT #18

This is one of my best turquoise glazes, and differs so slightly from its nearest competitors among my other, related, formulations that it will serve by itself as the type for all of them. At its best, it is a richly colored, vibrant blue with just a suspicion of green.

Empirical Formula	$.646\ Na_2O$	$.2983\ Al_2O_3$	$2.902\ SiO_2$
	$.09\ CaO$		
	$.264\ K_2O$		

Batch Recipe	Buckingham feldspar	157.34
	Flint	72.0
	Whiting	9.0
	Soda ash	68.47
		306.81
	Copper oxide (2% of batch)	6.17

Use of White Slip Under Turquoise Glaze

A good white slip is indispensable to achieving the turquoise color — either that, or a white porcelain body for the ware. Without such a white ground, the normal buff tones of a stoneware body will simply drown out the blueness of the color, turning it into a brownish green. The white slip, on the other hand, not only serves as a brightly reflective foil to the turquoise, but by its very composition aids it in the direction of the desired color. (See Chapter 11 for white slip recipes.)

Ideally, the slip should be first applied to the greenware when the latter is leatherhard, and then bisqued with it. (See "Use of White Slip under Copper Red Glazes" in Chapter 5, for a more detailed explanation.)

Another valuable aspect of the white slip is that it offers a perfect ground for black underglaze decorations which seem to intensify the visual appeal of the turquoise glaze itself. They can be brushed on the slip either before or after it has been bisqued with the ware. (The recipe for my black underglaze is given in Chapter 11.) It will be observed that AT#18, when properly applied and fired, causes no distortion in the outlines of the underglaze decoration.

Mixing the Glaze Ingredients. This glaze must be *dry*-milled. Follow the directions for dry-milling in Chapter 1.

Like the CR glazes, AT#18 tends to crystallize if kept in a wet condition too long. Thus, only so much glaze material as is to be used promptly should be mixed with the necessary water. Be sure to add the water in very small increments, stirring it into the glaze constantly, until the consistency is like that of very heavy cream. At this point, it is still not ready for use. Because of the large amount of soda ash in the glaze, it will at first seem thicker than it actually is, since a chemical reaction to the water will be taking place at that stage. Let the thickened glaze stand a while until it cools down (the soda ash interacting with the water will have warmed it up noticeably), and then add, very slowly, whatever slight extra water you may deem necessary to bring the glaze mix to a smoother flowing, easier to handle, yet still rather creamy consistency. Under no circumstances should you add so much water as to make the glaze mix thin and runny — a very easy mistake to make, owing to the great solubility of the soda ash content. Besides creating difficulties in application to the ware, such an over-thinned glaze will not yield a satisfactory turquoise color when fired. Nor is it possible to let the overthinned glaze stand and settle out, since there is really *no* "excess" water from a raw soda ash glaze that can be discarded without completely unbalancing the formulation of the glaze and, hence, the fired result.

On the subject of the water used in the glaze, it is most relevant at this point to remark on an interesting experiment I conducted with turquoise glazes and water from two different sources. It proved to be so significant that a brief account of it must be given here as essential information for the reader. My purpose was to discern the effects on glaze and glaze color, if any, of New York City water as compared with pure spring water of a sparkling clarity coming from veins in pegmatitic granite. Identical glazes, except for the differences in water, were used on similarly shaped pieces placed side by side in the same firing in various parts of an electric kiln. The contrasts created by the two waters were startling. Those glazes mixed with city water produced brilliant, clear turquoise blues; those mixed with the delicious spring water became dull, rather muddy green! The probable explanation of this phenomenon is that the spring water issuing from pegmatitic veins is overrich in alumina leached out of the mother rock, and, as I have already indicated, alumina is absolutely inimical to the turquoise color. In practical terms, then, the conclusion for the reader is obvious: if you hope to make turquoise glazes, and the water in your locality is "contaminated" with alumina, you had better use distilled water instead. It is also quite conceivable that the differing mineral contents of various waters will have serious impact on the colors and textures of such other glaze types as Chün, celadons, and copper reds.

Applying the Glaze. Follow the directions given in Chapter 1, except as otherwise indicated below. Special pains must be taken to avoid overwetting the ware; otherwise the drying glaze will almost certainly form hairline cracks and begin to peel.

As a corollary caution, I must also add that this type of turquoise glaze should ideally be applied *only by spraying*. For a time, I was quite mystified by the unsatisfactory color and texture of the insides of bowls and vases that I had glazed by *pouring*: they were usually rough and brownish green, most without even a hint of the lovely blue color on their outer surfaces to which, in contradistinction, the glaze had been applied by spraying. Then the thought occurred to me that the *physical* impact of pouring might be causing a partial assimilation of the alumina in the white slip to the superimposed glaze. An ensuing experiment dramatically proved this theory: after *pouring* the glaze into a ewer-shaped piece, I deliberately allowed some of it to run over part of the outside; I then wiped it off the outside, and proceeded to glaze the entire outside by *spraying* on the glaze as usual. The fired result: most of the ewer's outside was a lovely turquoise, with the exception of a quite green patch where the *poured* glaze had originally run over.

Drying the Glaze. Follow the directions given in Chapter 1. Be certain to allow the glaze enough time to become bone dry on the ware. If this is not done, premature firing will inevitably cause large patches of glaze to crawl and peel from the ware.

Firing the Glaze. This glaze requires an *oxidizing* fire to cones 7 or 7-plus. An electric kiln, of course, would be best for this purpose; but a gas-fired kiln can also be used, provided no reduction is permitted to take place at any time in the entire procedure. Either way, therefore, the firing process is the simplest thing about this glaze: a matter of steadily bringing the work-heat up to the desired cone in the presence of sufficient oxygen.

In Conclusion

The difficulties I have detailed concerning this lovely glaze provide us with additional, useful insights into some of the possible causes of the imperfect communication about glazes between potters far and wide. It is an all-too-common experience to obtain a formula for a fine glaze, either directly from a fellow potter or from a respected book, and then find that it just does not work out. At such times, one tends to blame oneself, or the other potter, or the pretensions of the book; but very likely, the fault may lie in such things as the firing characteristics of the kiln or, as I am now more strongly suggesting, the many subtly related considerations I have stressed in this chapter, such as the mineral content of the water one is using or the special techniques employed in glaze preparation and application. As I have tried to do throughout this book, all these things need to be carefully spelled out if a glaze recipe is to be of any use to another potter. The various factors that make a glaze perform at its beautiful best are very delicately balanced with each other; they require equally delicate handling.

7
TEMMOKU

Temmoku is actually the Japanese name for Chien ware, a type of brown or black slip-glazed stoneware brought to its greatest perfection in Fukien province during the Sung era. The term has also been extended to cover other varieties of similar type that were made in Kiangsi and Honan provinces at about the same time. All these wares have dark, iron-rich glazes that take a number of different forms or patterns, including such famous ones as "oil spot," "tea dust," and "hare's fur."

The genesis of these glazes may well have been the observations made by ancient Chinese potters who had accidentally overfired red earthenware pots with the result that the pots had not only slumped very badly but had become vitreous through and through. Some (as I have seen in my own incautious experiments) may have turned into veritable glossy puddles. Sooner or later, such experiences would have urged experimentation with the clay body material as a glaze, instead, at higher-than-earthenware temperatures. For essentially, temmoku is high-fired stoneware glazed with earthenware clay that fluxes almost too easily to be any good even as an earthenware clay body.

The glazes in this chapter have as their original starting point a formulation developed by my friend David Holleman and offered to me with a generous supply of one component essential to all of them. This material is *red slate powder* obtained a good many years ago by Mr. Holleman from a source in Granville, New York, the site of the red slate deposits. Originally, efforts had been made to use this material as a clay body, but they proved unrewarding. Later, experiment with the red slate by Mr. Holleman for glaze purposes yielded a good temmoku, sometimes with the oil spot characteristic. My work with this material has been extensive, and has produced a wide variety of temmoku types, including oil spot, deep black, dark brown, tea dust, and hare's fur. Some of these glazes are best in oxidation firings; others, in reduction. This distinction should be carefully noted as it occurs in each case.

Oil Spot and Deep Black

The oil spot phenomenon is manifested as a great number of bright, round, silvery spots of varying sizes that appear to be floating on the surface of the brown-black glaze matrix. These spots are created in the course of the firing of the glaze by a series of developments: (1) Bubbles rising through the molten glaze reach the surface and burst there, leaving pits or craters in the surface at those points. (2) As the firing continues, the more soluble and therefore more fluid, extra iron-rich portions of the surrounding glaze pour into these pits and fill them before larger-particled, less soluble portions of the glaze can move to them. (3) As a result, when the firing is concluded at just the right stage, the pits are more or less filled with the extra iron-rich glaze material that has crystallized into patterns which are more reflective of light than the rest of the glaze.

It is interesting and instructive to observe, with the aid of a magnifying hand lens, that the entire surface of such a glaze is actually still quite bumpy with only partly smoothed-over pit edges; even more interesting, each seeming oil spot is formed by grayish metallic streaks or lines that radiate outwards in a crystalline pattern from a central point to the limits of the former pit. Similar examination of the same glaze fired to a higher cone reveals the disappearance of both the pits and the crystals, resulting in a black or brown glaze *without* oil spots. The additional liquefaction of all the glaze material at a greater work-heat has thus produced a more uniform mix of the molten glaze and has thereby erased all distinction between the matrix and the pits holding their special iron-rich material.

Implicit in the above description is a caution about care in observing the firing procedures outlined later on in this section.

Two of my best oil spot glazes will suffice here.

T+C6

When applied and fired correctly, this glaze will often yield a beautiful, but somewhat fine-spotted oil spot. At higher temperatures, it becomes a smooth, dark, glossy black rather more like some of the Ch'ing "mirror blacks," though softer and more unctuous. One additional advance point of prime importance: if used on certain stoneware bodies with a high silica content, like my Stoneware Body #4, this glaze has a tendency to chip off on the lips of some pieces and even to dunt the entire ware; it fits perfectly, however, without either of these faults, on my Stoneware Body #8. (See Chapter 11 for stoneware body recipes.)

The following empirical formula is a purely hypothetical one, which I have worked out and used simply as a helpful basis for further experiment. It is not offered as accurate, since it fails to represent the invaluable impurities (like iron oxides, manganese, sulphates, etc.) in the red slate powder that possibly make it so superior to substances like Albany slip, Barnard clay, and other secondary clays with which I have experimented for this purpose less successfully.

Empirical Formula $.25\ K_2O$ $2.315\ Al_2O_3$ $5.682\ SiO_2$

$.75\ CaO$ $?\ Fe_2O_3$, etc.

Batch Recipe	Red slate powder	65.
	Georgia kaolin	5.
	Buckingham feldspar	20.
	Whiting	10.
		100.
	Cobalt oxide (1% of batch)	1.

T+C6 cc mg

This glaze was developed in order to overcome a slight tendency on the part of T+C6 to crawl unless due care is taken with its application and drying. One cause of this problem with T+C6 is the unusually large proportion of raw clay-like materials employed. I was therefore prompted to create a series of *calcined* clay glazes so as to diminish the amount of chemically bonded water in the glaze components and thereby lessen the chance of loading the ware with too much H_2O when applying the glaze. TC+6 cc mg is probably the best of the series. It has a somewhat more unctuous quality than does T+C6, and is easier to handle.

Calcining Clay-Like Materials

The raw powdered material (like kaolin or red slate powder) should be placed in a previously bisqued but unglazed pot, and then bisqued along with other greenware. After the firing, the material may be emptied into a kitchen sieve and rubbed through it into a fine powder. This will be very easy to do, since most of the material will still be powdery after the firing, with only a few lumps here and there.

In arriving at the batch recipe below, only .22 molecular equivalents of *raw* red slate powder, calculated with the equivalent weight of Al_2O_3, were utilized; 1.6775 molecular equivalents of *calcined* red slate were calculated as *calcined* Al_2O_3. (For a comprehensive explanation of how to convert empirical formulas into batch weights or recipes, see Chapter 12.)

Hypothetical Empirical Formula	.25 K_2O	2.0325 Al_2O_3	5.682 SiO_2
	.53 CaO	? Fe_2O_3, etc.	
	.22 MgO		

Batch Recipe	Whiting	53.0
	Magnesium carbonate	18.48
	Buckingham feldspar	149.0
	Calcined Georgia kaolin	29.97
	Raw red slate powder	56.76
	Calcined red slate powder	372.4
		679.61
	Cobalt oxide (1% of batch)	6.79

Mixing the Glaze Ingredients in T+C6 and T+C6 cc mg. Follow the directions given in Chapter 1. *Wet*-milling will be necessary. (Large quantities of clay-like substances have a tendency to pack down and not mix sufficiently with the other ingredients during dry-milling.) About half an hour of milling will be sufficient, since too fine a particle size is undesirable, especially for the oil spot effect.

Applying the Glaze. Follow the directions given in Chapter 1. It is very important to use as little water as possible in the glaze mix when applying it, since overwetting the ware will be certain to cause crawling. For the same reason, adjust your spray gun to as dry an atomization as possible, but be sure to apply a thick coat of glaze to the ware; oil spots do not form in thin-layered glaze applications. In so doing, however, be most careful not to saturate the ware to the point where, as it builds up on the ware, the applied glaze begins to look shiny; otherwise, it will probably develop hairline cracks later and will then peel in the firing. (Ironically, the parts that do peel, in such instances, fold over onto other glaze portions, and because of the thereby multiplied thickness of the glaze at these points, develop handsome, large oil spots! The only trouble is that these passages directly adjoin ugly bald spots.)

Drying the Glaze. Follow the directions given in Chapter 1. Be sure that both glaze and ware are bone dry before firing.

Firing Procedures. For the oil spot effect, these glazes must be fired in an *oxidizing* atmosphere to no more than cone 8, preferably a trifle less. An electric kiln is ideal for the purpose, though a gas kiln may also serve, provided there be no reduction whatever during the firing process.

For the glossy, deep black effect, the oxidation firing may be carried to a full cone 8 and held there to soak for about three-quarters of an hour. With an electric kiln this can be done by shutting off only half of the switches during the soaking period, or by leaving all of them on at the *low* setting for the same period. In a gas kiln, the oxidation firing can be allowed to progress to cone 9 before shut-off.

Placement in the kiln, of course, represents another method of control in choosing between the oil spot and glossy, deep black effects. As I have noted in earlier chapters, the lowest and uppermost areas of the kiln are usually the coolest and may sometimes be as much as one cone lower than the middle areas by the end of the firing. Thus, in a full cone 8 oxidation firing with a soaking period added to achieve the glossy, dark black effect, very satisfactory oil spots may also be produced on pots placed either on the floor or in the topmost levels of the kiln.

Dark Brown Jemmoku

One glaze will serve for this section. It represents a kind of transition between the previous glazes and those that follow later. Even with the same proportion of cobalt added, the color is a brown of great depth and richness, rather than a black. The presence of wood ash in the formulation probably accounts for this quality, as well as for the increased translucency which tends to give a contrasting thinness of color to the lips of fired ware. Scattered through the brown matrix are very tiny, barely discernible pinpoints of yellow, a characteristic that will be more fully developed in the succeeding sections of this chapter.

In those firings that end somewhat below cone 8, the glaze takes on something of the appearance of T+C6 oil spot: the brown is nearer a black, and there is the suggestion of scattered, silvery iridescence from exceptionally small oil spot crystals. When markedly underfired, say, at cone 7, it emerges from the kiln exactly the same in appearance as the so-called "lizard skin" glaze which, as Hetherington points out, is simply a typical form of *underfired* temmoku.

Batch Recipe for	Red slate powder	62.
T+CA72	Georgia kaolin	4.
	Buckingham feldspar	13.5
	Whiting	3.5
	Softwood ash	17.
		100.0
	Cobalt oxide (1% of batch)	1.0

Procedures. Follow the directions given above in this chapter for the two previous glazes, T+C6 and T+C6 cc mg. The oxidation firing should go to a full cone 8 with an additional soaking period of about three-quarters of an hour.

Tea Dust or Yellow-Spotted Brown Temmoku

The glazes in this and the next section involve a radical reshuffling of the components of the parent temmoku, together with some substitution and omission. All omit the kaolin and substitute a soda spar like Maine feldspar for the Buckingham feldspar. The proportion of red slate powder is also significantly reduced. The results are: (1) a much greater ease of handling these preparations in application and firing; (2) increased fluidity of the glaze at cones 8 through 10; and (3) the presence of yellow spots owing to the extra surcharge of iron oxides in the mixture, and in the case of some fired to cone 10 — as will be noted in the later section below — yellow streaks in the matrix of deep, rich brown.

It should be stressed that the five glazes detailed in this section are described here only as they appear after an oxidation firing to cone 8.

T#2

When fully fired, this brown glaze exhibits scattered yellow spots in the form of fine dots that are appreciably larger than the pinpoints of yellow in T+CA72. The yellow color of the dots is also somewhat grayed. Sometimes these dots are so closely bunched that on vertical surfaces they seem to form a drizzle-like pattern anticipating hare's fur.

Batch Recipe	Red slate powder	50.
	Maine feldspar	35.
	Whiting	15.
		100.
	Red iron oxide (5% of batch)	5.

T#10

Here the yellow spots are larger and more closely and evenly distributed through the glaze than in T#2.

Batch Recipe	Red slate powder	46.
	Maine feldspar	35.
	Whiting	19.
		100.
	Red iron oxide (5% of batch)	5.

T#14

This is probably the most beautiful, and as will be seen later, the most versatile of these glazes. The yellow specks are larger, but not patchy, and they are abundantly distributed throughout the matrix of the glaze in such a way as not to diminish the depth and translucency of the dark, rich brown itself.

Batch Recipe	Red slate powder	43.
	Maine feldspar	35.
	Whiting	22.
		100.
	Red iron oxide (7% of batch)	7.

T#16

Here we have an adjustment of the preceding glaze formulation to accommodate the presence of wood ash. The result is a very dark brown, lustrous glaze of rich texture containing isolated spots of vivid bright yellow. The general impression is of a starlit night in which the black has strangely gone brown. The fluidity of the glaze tends to drain the color at the lips of the ware to somewhat lighter, unspeckled brown that is also more translucent.

Examination of the larger spots on this glaze with a high-powered hand lens is especially informative. The spots reveal themselves as being more or less uniformly constructed crystals, each one radiating outwards like so many close-packed flower petals from a central point. Like the somewhat similar crystals seen in the oil spot glaze, their facets are additionally reflective of light; unlike them, they are a reddish yellow color, instead of a grayish silver. Scattered elsewhere in the matrix around these relatively large crystal flower forms are many other, much smaller, yellow spots that do not seem to have achieved (or perhaps, retained) crystalline structure nor, in some cases, quite to have reached the glaze surface. All in all, then, the tea dust glaze emerges as a special variety of so-called crystalline glaze.

Batch Recipe	Red slate powder	42.
	Maine feldspar	32.
	Whiting	21.
	Softwood ash	5.
		100.
	Red iron oxide (7% of batch)	7.

T#20

This section of our chapter concludes with another excellent tea dust, in which the specks are very large and handsome, and tend to become more closely bunched as the glaze drains towards the center of the ware. The matrix, which is a rich, reddish dark brown, is not so fluid and glossy as in T#16 and therefore leaves a thicker, slightly less translucent covering at the lip of the pot. The magnified view of the yellow spots reveals marked differences from those seen in T#16. The crystalline pattern of the large spots is much less regular and contained. The radiating "petals" are more ragged and randomly curved; and their color, as well as the center point, is appreciably darker and less reflective. The number of small, uncrystallized spots also floating in the matrix is larger.

In the composition given below, it will be noted that T#20 departs from all the other glazes in this chapter in its inclusion of flint in the formulation.

Batch Recipe	Red slate powder	40.
	Maine feldspar	32.
	Whiting	19.
	Flint	9.
		100.
	Red iron oxide (7% of batch)	7.

Procedures for the Tea Dust Temmoku Glazes. Follow the directions for mixing, applying, drying, and firing given above in this chapter under T+C6 and T+C6 cc mg. Before applying the glaze, you may choose to intensify the usual dark brown to almost a black, without lessening any other qualities of these glazes, by first applying a good wash of black iron oxide in water to the ware. To insure a better bond between the iron wash and the clay body, it would be best to do this on the leatherhard greenware before bisquing it, though application to bisqued ware will also work. In addition, for aesthetic reasons it is a good idea to coat the underside, or foot, of the ware with a thin wash of black iron oxide. Thus, an otherwise buff or gray body will be brought into fuller harmony with the iron-rich glaze covering the rest of it.

In applying the glaze be careful, as usual, to avoid the extremes of excessively thick or thin coatings. The former will produce a rather opaque, overall tan effect of no great distinction, in which the dots of yellow are all merged into one sheet of dull color. The other extreme of too thin an application will produce a rich enough, rather watery dark brown, but it will contain few or none of the yellow dots.

For the tea dust, spotted effect, all these glazes require a full cone 8 oxidation firing. T#16 and T#20 will also work quite well as tea dust glazes in a reduction firing to as much as cone 9. (For reduction firing procedures, see the directions given in Chapter 1.)

Hare's Fur, Partridge Feather, or Streaked Temmoku

All but one of the glazes treated under this heading are almost identical in formulation with several of those detailed in the previous section. Their chief distinguishing characteristic is the pattern of streaks created by firing the ware to cone 10 in a reducing atmosphere.

When seen in the mass, these fine-lined streaks are suggestive of the close-packed hairs of smooth animal fur; hence, the traditional name, "hare's fur." Actual close examination of the glaze surface under sufficient magnification shows, however, that the apparent streaks, or "hairs," are really separate yellow or light brown spots and crystals that have been more straightly aligned by the downward flow of the more molten matrix surrounding them. The lines are really not half so continuous and regular as they seem to the naked eye. In fact, they are broken patterns of separate clots and amorphous crystals that have become arranged in irregular lines above one another for fairly limited distances in the glaze. On either side of this haphazard column of yellow or light brown dots is an equally irregular area of glossy, very dark brown or black-brown glaze. This dark "background line" contrasts with the "dotted-column line," and together with myriad other such side-by-side arrangements in the glaze, emphasizes the impression of hairs. In the case of the so-called "partridge feather" variation, good numbers of larger yellow crystals retain their identity and form, and stand out in the columnar flow of the smaller and relatively amorphous dots. Macroscopically, therefore, the resulting pattern seems to contain larger "eyes" among the streaks and lines, thereby resembling the patterns of certain bird feathers.

Thus, from this magnified view of the streaked, hare's fur glazes, we realize that they are really varieties of the tea dust or spotted glazes made more fluid by higher work-heats.

I should point out that my hare's fur glaze effects are finer lined than those in the classic Chien ware. The color of their lines is also a more yellowish light brown; in the authentic Sung hare's fur, the streaks are a grayer, more subtly muted light brown.

T#2

When reduction fired to cone 10, especially over a black iron oxide wash, this glaze develops a kind of very thin-lined, light brown streaked pattern that suggests the visual impression of a fine, light rain. Where the streaks come closest together, the color sometimes shifts from yellow to gray. The background color is both more matte and bluer black than it is in oxidation firing.

Use the batch recipe for T#2 given earlier in this chapter.

T#14Co

Owing to the greater fluidity of this glaze, the streaks give the illusion of being more continuous from top to bottom of the ware than they are in T#2. This impression is brought out more strongly by the flow of the thick, viscous glaze matrix towards the foot of the ware. The matrix itself is a rich, very dark brown made even darker and more lustrous by the addition of cobalt oxide to the glaze mixture. The total effect, which is most strongly reminiscent of smooth animal fur, marks this as probably the best of my hare's fur approximations.

Follow the batch recipe for T#14 given earlier in this chapter. *Add 1% of cobalt oxide to the batch.*

T#16

Identical in formulation with its spotted, oxidized counterpart, this glaze can also produce the type of partridge feather streaked effect already described. The only difference is the process of firing the glaze to cone 10 in a reducing atmosphere.

Use the batch recipe for T#16 given earlier in this chapter.

T#15

The final entry for this group is a glaze that is *markedly* more fluid than any of the preceding three. As a result, the streaks are very much more pronounced and numerous, and they therefore tend to give the ware a more yellow-brown overall appearance, though the glaze matrix is still a quite dark brown. On rounded bottle forms, the upper surfaces that curve somewhat towards the horizontal often retain numbers of large, yellow crystals that give those portions a slightly more "partridge feather" look. Special attention must be given to the procedural directions below.

Batch Recipe		
	Red slate powder	40.
	Georgia kaolin	4.
	Maine feldspar	34.
	Whiting	22.
		100.
	Red iron oxide (9% of batch)	9.

Procedures for the Hare's Fur and Partridge Feather Glazes. Follow the directions for mixing, applying, drying, and firing given above in this chapter under T+C6 and T+C6 cc mg, as well as the additional directions indicated in the previous section on tea dust glazes.

In applying these glazes for the hare's fur effect, the same additional advice is particularly relevant. For example, excessively thick application will in effect obscure the hoped-for streaks and will produce a glaze whose entire surface becomes one dull tan mass. The latter danger is especially true of the inner surfaces of bowls, as the resultant yellowish pooling is extremely opaque, dry-looking, and generally unattractive. T#15 requires particularly careful handling in this regard; for this glaze it would generally be better to err on the side of applying too little glaze than too much.

A most important extra caution concerning these hare's fur glazes: when fired as required to cone 10, they become so much more fluid that if proper care is not taken, the glaze will tend to flow off the lowest portions of the ware onto the shelf. It is therefore *absolutely necessary* to leave the foot and bottom area of the bisqued ware quite free of glaze. Thus, when first spraying glaze on the lower and outer surfaces of an inverted piece, as described in Chapter 1, be sure to use a circular glaze-baffle made of linoleum that is cut much larger in diameter than the actual size of the ware's foot ring. This extra-large linoleum circle should be positioned over the foot ring so that it extends evenly at least 2″ outwards from the ring in all directions. In this way, it will prevent sprayed glaze from reaching, not only the foot, but also at least 1″ or 2″ of the outer surfaces just above the foot. As an extra means to this end, hold the spray gun well above and to one side of the inverted piece and angle it more or less *downwards*; thus, the glaze will be unable to settle on those areas adjacent to the foot that are shielded by the linoleum baffle, but will reach the rest of the pot's outer surfaces. Finally, a straight-edged wooden modeling tool may be used to scrape away any stray bits of glaze that may have reached these areas adjacent to the foot. Simply turn the banding wheel with the inverted glazed piece still in place and remove the unwanted glaze with the cutting edge of the tool gently pressed against the ware. Finish off this clean-up process with a dry sponge to dust off any remaining glaze specks. In so doing, be careful not to remove the wash of black iron oxide previously applied to the same area. It can, of course, be retouched if any of the wash is lost to the glaze clean-up process.

In firing these glazes, follow the steps given in Chapter 1 for reduction firing to cone 10. In the case of T#15, however, a somewhat lower final work-heat would be preferable. This can be best achieved either by firing to no more than cone 9 or, if in the same cone 10 firings with the other hare's fur glazes, by judicious placement of the T#15-glazed wares at either the lowest or the topmost levels of the kiln.

8
TZ'U-CHOU

One of the most beautiful of Sung stonewares is the Tz'u-chou of Hopei province. Despite its great dignity, elegance, and grace, as well as the infinite pains that unavoidably must have gone into creating and decorating individual pieces, a dubious tradition has it that these were meant to be merely "people's ware." At the other pole, supposedly, would be Kuan ware for "palace use" exclusively. This snobbish distinction, if ever historically true, has since become meaningless. In the long run, the more important distinctions of aesthetic truth are quite outside history, having little or nothing to do with social distinctions as such. T'zu-chou wares would be at home wherever the taste and sensitivity needed to appreciate them happen to be. Like the best in all great art, their vigorous, masterly style transcends temporal considerations.

Of the several different varieties of T'zu-chou wares created in Sung times, the one that has most appeal to me is that which employs handsome brushwork decoration on a ground of white slip, with a thin, clear glaze covering both. (The brush-decorated turquoise wares described in Chapter 6 also belong to this type.) The attempt to achieve the right combination of these three factors raises several problems. The chief of these is to find a glaze or glazes that will: (1) permit a clear view of the decoration under the glaze; (2) not cause the decoration to bleed or run; and (3) maintain the rich, black tones of the underglaze. Paradoxically, after much experiment with new formulations that were something less than ideal, the thought occurred to me of trying some of my Lung-ch'üan and Chün glazes *without* iron oxide or yellow ochre. As I had hoped, several of these were satisfactory. Also, each had slightly different qualities from the others, so that all together they offer a good range of possibilities suiting the purpose.

Though most typically these glazes are colorless, it would be erroneous to give the impression that they are invariably so. I have already remarked on the relevancy of turquoise glazes to this type. I should also add that such a glaze as ACGW4-F3 *with* iron can be used as a very attractive celadon covering for brushwork, as indeed celadons were used with certain Tz'u-chou wares. (Another celadon glaze that adapts well to this purpose is CEL#11.) The emphasis in this chapter, however, is meant to show how the black-on-*white*-ground effect might be best achieved today.

Use of White Slip under the Glaze

For the Tz'u-chou effect with all these glazes, a white slip should be applied to the greenware before bisquing. (See Chapter 6 for a detailed account.)

On-Glaze Decoration

Besides the more classically authentic approach of underglaze decoration, brush painting *on* the unfired glaze can also produce very handsome effects. Any of the glazes in this chapter can be used as a base for on-glaze decoration; at cones 8 and 9, the fired result has an especially rich black, sharply defined quality. In this connection, it should be added that an aqueous suspension of plain yellow ochre can also be used for brushed on-glaze effects; it yields lighter, tan-yellow brushstrokes that lend variety and contrast to the underglaze black. The on-glaze approach is equally attractive on such other glaze surfaces as, for example, the microcrystalline matte of ACW-H1 mentioned in Chapter 3, when the latter is oxidation fired to cone 8 at most. Brushwork with underglaze black and with yellow ochre blends in particularly well with the soft, ivory-white background.

CIH-XF

This glaze is identical in its four essential components with the light blue Chün, CIH-p, except for the omission of the yellow ochre. Because of its wood ash (and, therefore, phosphorus) content, it has a slight tendency to become rather cloudy if applied too thickly. Also, because of its innately bluish celadon capabilities, too thick a coat, especially when most heavily reduced, will also give a faintly blue cast to the ware as a whole and to the black underglaze decoration in particular. Otherwise, with only a thin or medium-thick application to the ware, it functions very well as a clear, colorless glaze over a well-defined, rich black underglaze on white slip.

Batch Recipe	Buckingham feldspar	56.
	Flint	22.
	Whiting	13.
	Softwood ash	9.
		100.

ACGW-H4

This is a repeat of a Lung-ch'üan formulation, but with the omission of the black iron oxide. Unlike CIH-XF, this glaze is completely colorless at all times. At cone 10 with heavy reduction, it becomes a clear and glossy transparent on the white ground; at cone 8, it merges into a kind of semi-matte harmony with the white slip. It consistently brings out the full blackness of the underglaze in sharp definition.

Empirical Formula	.7572 CaO	.375 Al_2O_3	2.85 SiO_2
	.1135 MgO		
	.1291 K_2O		

Batch Recipe	Whiting	75.72
	Magnesium carbonate	9.53
	Buckingham feldspar	76.94
	Georgia kaolin	59.13
	Flint	93.44
		314.76

ACG7

In its celadon form, this glaze appears in Chapter 3 under the heading of Northern Celadons. As in the case of the previous two glazes in the present chapter, the only difference here lies in the omission of the black iron oxide from the batch recipe. Like them, it performs very effectively as a covering for black underglaze decorative treatment on white slip, retaining fairly good definition of the brushwork even on vertical surfaces. In texture, it is about halfway between ACGW-H4 and CIH-XF, being somewhat richer and deeper than the former and never as cloudy or blue as the latter may become on occasion.

Batch Recipe	Whiting	22.
	Magnesium carbonate	3.
	Buckingham feldspar	23.
	Georgia kaolin	18.
	Flint	28.
	Softwood ash	6.
		100.

ACG8

This excellent glaze is an exact repeat from the chapter on celadons, no additional iron having been employed there, either. The same qualities of slight unctuousness and wide firing range noted in connection with its use as a Lung-ch'üan glaze are equally characteristic here. Over white slip, it is fully translucent and reveals very sharply defined black underglaze brush decorations with no distortion of either color or outline.

Batch Recipe	Whiting	17.
	Magnesium carbonate	2.
	Buckingham feldspar	36.
	Georgia kaolin	12.
	Flint	27.
	Softwood ash	6.
		100.

FP#5b

The final glaze in this chapter has not been mentioned before. Strictly speaking, it is not a purely Tz'u-chou style glaze, since it has a tendency toward opaqueness if used in even moderately thick application. It is therefore not perfectly suited as an overlay for underglaze brushwork. However, I have consistently used it as a medium for *on*-glaze black decoration with excellent results. In combination with bisqued white slip, it offers a beautiful surface for this type of treatment, and creates the best of blacks with my regular black "underglaze." Its composition is typically of the "porcelain" variety with a high lime and magnesium content, and it offers a good range from cones 8 through 10.

Empirical Formula	.25 K_2O	.75 Al_2O_3	5.10 SiO_2
	.37 CaO		
	.38 MgO		

Batch Recipe	Buckingham feldspar	149.0
	Whiting	37.0
	Magnesium carbonate	31.92
	Kaolin	120.61
	Flint	153.15
		491.68

Procedures for Tz'u-chou Glazes. Follow the directions for mixing, applying, drying, and firing given in Chapter 1. See also the additional points made in Chapter 3 under procedures for the ACG Lung-ch'üan glazes.

Since clear, sharp definition of the underglaze brushstrokes is our goal here, rather than depth of glaze, apply the glaze in a relatively thin coating.

Firing may be either oxidation to cone 8 or reduction from cone 8 to cone 10, giving a range of surface from more or less semi-matte to glossy, fully transparent.

9
GLAZES IN COMBINATION

Inevitably, the spirit of investigation and experiment that produced the glazes detailed in the previous chapters led to attempts to use some of these glazes in combination with each other. In fact, it was in just such fashion that glazes like C+GA1F1 and CEL#7, for example, were started on their way. A few illustrative words, therefore, are in order on the special effects gained from a few glaze combinations.

Probably the most exciting couple of glazes I have used in combination, especially on tall bottles, are the unmilled form of CIH-p (the light blue Chün type) and T#14Co (a hare's fur temmoku). (Their recipes are given in Chapters 1 and 7, respectively.) The two basic methods of employing them together are, simply put, one-over-the-other and side-by-side.

One-Over-the-Other Combinations of CIH-p and T#14Co

When a pot first glazed with a full, thick coating of CIH-p is oversprayed with T#14Co, several different effects may be obtained. If the T#14Co overspray is relatively light, the result will be a mottling faintly reminiscent of the "egg shell" surface of a salt glaze, but with a clear distinction between the brown flecks of the T#14Co and the stony matte celadon, plus the Chün blue passages that more typically occur as part of the CIH-p background. If the T#14Co overspray is heavier, the result is a rich, glossy brown with runs and mottlings of bright blue Chün showing through.

This latter general effect can be further varied, in an especially interesting way, by reserving predesigned areas on the pot for the application of only the T#14Co glaze. That is, if paper resists are used during the application of the CIH-p glaze, certain areas may be kept free of it; then, when the paper resists are removed, these areas, together with the rest of the pot already covered with CIH-p, are exposed to a full coating of T#14Co. This technique employs both one-over-the-other and side-by-side applications. The result is a beautiful patterning of the final glaze with purely typical hare's fur yellow-streaked "lines" running down into the other, combined glaze areas.

Side-by-Side Combinations of CIH-p and T#14Co

Purely side-by-side application can be achieved in two different ways, with correspondingly different effects. One is to control the initial spraying or dipping of the first glaze so as to leave certain areas of the pot bare for the later application of the other glaze, which should overlap it a little for enrichment and shading off. The other method, with equally striking results, is again to use paper resists during the CIH-p application in whatever patterns one thinks best, and then to fill in these patterns later with the T#14Co only slightly overlapping the CIH-p. In this method, then, the T#14Co is *not* applied to the entire pot, but only to limited areas. When concentric-circle or spiral resists are employed, the mixed effects of Chün blue, gray stony celadon, and yellow-streaked temmoku draining into each other often produce wildly fantastic shapes and patterns.

Use of Masking Tape for Resists

Perhaps a word about the paper resists themselves would be helpful. Ordinary paper cut to desired patterns may serve, but there is the problem of getting it to adhere adequately to the ware during the first glaze spraying. Gum tragacanth, corn syrup, or honey may be used as a temporary bond. However, the most useful material I have found for this purpose is masking tape, especially in its widest dimensions. I overlap one piece of it on another to make a sufficiently large square or oblong, draw a pattern on it, and then cut out the pattern with scissors. The resulting design is then pressed into place on the ware. As soon as the first coating of glaze is applied to the whole pot, the masking tape pattern can be removed, loosening it first at one edge or corner with a sharp-pointed tool like a scribe or large needle. What is left is a bare pattern on the pot which can then be coated with a second glaze.

Copper Red as On-Glaze Decoration

One other glaze-on-glaze combination should be singled out for description, especially as it is in keeping with a beautifully effective Sung precedent. That is the use of copper-red decoration on Chün, as mentioned in passing earlier in this book. Such freely brushed splashes or carefully spaced "blushes" are often found on Chün ware; and in many cases so overrun the entire surface of the glaze (as, for example in most of the specimens in the Fogg Museum collection) that they have misled some connoisseurs into thinking copper oxide to be the source of the *blue* in all Chün ware. The truth is that copper oxide, tending to be more volatile at higher temperatures, can easily suffuse the surface of nearby glaze areas from other areas intended for only limited decoration with copper, and can thus lead even careful chemical analysts to wrong conclusions about the basic glaze composition. In any case, Hetherington has effectively laid to rest, through a combination of judicious chemical analysis and keen insights, the notion entertained by some that copper is in any way responsible for the *blue* color in Chün. My own exhaustive experiments with both iron and copper in phosphorus-bearing feldspathic glazes completely bear out his findings. But to return to the glaze-on-glaze effect of copper-red decoration on Chün: the basic glaze is usually CIH-p, or, on occasion, CIW-p milled. Over this glaze, already thickly applied to the ware, I freely splash a copper-red design, using a Chinese brush heavily loaded with CR 16b. Since CR 16b has a strong tendency to run freely during the firing, a quality that is also intensified by the fluxing power of the CIH-p under it, it is wisest to use this combination on relatively horizontal surfaces, such as large platters or shallow bowls.

Another effective copper on-glaze technique is to brush designs, or spray areas, *very lightly* with plain copper carbonate in water-and-corn-syrup over such already applied glazes as CIW-p milled, KCC#3, or G#6. The outcome is often a charming pink "blush," or with the brush technique, a mixture of pink, blue, green, and even tan against the rich green celadon background. Avoid too heavy an application of the copper, or the desired colors will be lost and, instead, a blackish gunmetal effect will be the result.

Other Combinations

Other one-over-the-other or side-by-side combinations of glaze will inevitably occur to the adventurous potter. For example, a viscous white glaze like SK#1 offers possibilities for a heightened decorative touch when added in one or two places over the CIH-m and T#14Co combinations. Where thickly and judiciously applied as a third glaze, it both stands out and blends in quite attractively at the edges with the other two glazes.

A particularly striking combination of T#14Co and wet-milled CIH-p I have developed is produced using the following process: First, I glaze the entire piece with a good, no more than medium-thick coating of T#14Co. Then, when the glaze and ware are dry enough to handle, but not yet bone dry, I make a pattern of small (*not* tiny) dots of varying sizes in the glaze covering by removing, right down to the surface of the bisque, the coating of T#14Co with any small, sharp-pointed instrument (like a scribe). Finally, with a small, fine-pointed brush, I refill the empty dots with sufficient amounts of wet-milled CIH-p to bring the new glaze up to and a little bit over the level of the surrounding T#14Co.

When fired under full reduction to cone 10, the piece will have become a fine hare's fur with an especially attractive pattern of light blue Chün or gray-green Kuan spots or both. The proximity of the CIH-p spots and the surrounding T#14Co produces handsome effects. The spots, partly circled by a fine, dark brown line, turn colors ranging from gray-green to light blue and, in some cases, lapis lazuli. The immediately contiguous portions of the hare's fur glaze, especially just below the spots, develop subtle dark brown tones shading back into the surrounding hare's fur. The overall effect possesses a most unusual beauty.

It is worth noting that this effect has a marked resemblance to the so-called "yao pien" (or "kiln transmutation") phenomenon described rather mysteriously by both Koyama-Figgess and Hayashiga-Hasebe (see *Bibliography*). According to the latter, who call the phenomenon by its Japanese name, "yohen," there are only three specimens of this ware preserved in Japan, and none in China, Europe, or America. They add: "These are not only the most beautiful of the Chien wares, but are without doubt among the finest ceramics made on this earth at any time." Great praise, indeed! The best one of the three extant specimens is pictured in a color plate in the handsome book by Koyama and Figgess. A small bowl less than five inches in diameter and under three inches in height, it is a truly remarkable masterpiece. The basic color is apparently a deep blackish brown temmoku, which is beautifully decorated with what seem to be Chün-blue clusters of spots that are not only darkly outlined (like mine), but also seem to float in a nearby haze of light blue in the surrounding brown. Koyama and Figgess describe these spots as "gleaming with dark-blue, bluish-green, lapis lazuli, and silver iridescence." Personally, I find it hard to believe that only one glaze is involved in the making of this fine bowl. Two contrasting glazes such as I have employed would explain the phenomenon more instructively than the mystic implications of "kiln transmutation," which, after all, seems only to be another way of saying the more familiar "kiln reduction."

Firing Procedures

All the glazes-in-combination described above are customarily fired with full reduction as detailed in Chapter 1 to cone 10; but there is no reason to suggest that similar combinations of other types are not effective in oxidation firings.

10
ADVENTURES WITH OLD AND NEW GLAZES

Although every one of the glazes and techniques described in these pages has yielded numerous stoneware pots of the hues and textures indicated, and has thus been more or less "true to type," it would be inaccurate to imply that such results have been invariable. The very nature of pottery, with its many contributing, diverse elements, prevents that conclusion. As I have already made clear, not all my Chün pots have been blue, any more than were the green, or indeed brownish green, ones of Sung times; nor have all my copper reds been dark, rich oxbloods or delicately shaded peach blooms. And my own advice, so freely given to the reader of this book, has not consistently saved numbers of my own temmoku pieces from erupting into dull, uniform tans of crystallized iron, thus obscuring the desired hare's fur streaks. Such is the lot of the potter who refuses to sit down safely with the "one or two glazes" enjoined on him by conventional dictate. But it is a lot that encompasses not only desperation and frustration, but also endless charm and excitement. I find it somehow particularly fascinating that the unique qualities of a special beauty, once analyzed, pinned down, and completely achieved, can still elude me the next time around. The successes of the past do not insure constant duplication in the future. In fact, some seem to be lost forever. They are irreducible mysteries — until suddenly a solution suggests itself, and works.

KCC+Y2: The Story of a Glaze Type Never Created Before

One glaze stands out in my experience as having promised to be a perpetual, invincible challenge. And for almost eight years it kept that promise. Paradoxically, this elusive glaze revealed its full loveliness with its very first firing; and successive firings not too long after from the same batch were also rather satisfactory, though not to the same extent as in the beginning. But after a lapse of time, and for a very long period thereafter, I was unable to achieve the same effect with this glaze, an effect I have thus far never seen on other ceramics, ancient or modern.

Now, the special characteristics of this desired effect are: (1) a rich brown background color; (2) a somewhat glossy, fatty texture full of rather large bubbles and covered with very tiny, healed-over pitmarks; and (3), the most distinguishing feature, a *cerulaean blue* "oil spot" effect collecting in hundreds of these little pits. On some of the pots fired during the initial experiment, some of the pit colors were also a golden brown, instead of blue; in the slightly later firings the background color was a lighter brown than formerly. Stranger still, in the much later firings made from the same batch after the wet glaze had "aged" in its jar several months, a rather dark, unctuous *celadon* without any pits or blue spots was the result.

At this point, my troubles with KCC+Y2 began. Again and again, fresh attempts with new batch after new batch of the same glaze yielded only variations of the celadon, without a sign of the amazing blue oil spot effect. Ringing the changes on reduction firing schedules was also unproductive in recreating the tantalizing lost glaze. The mystery seemed to be insoluble. Would I have to call it "kiln transmutation," and let it go at that?

But meanwhile the story had not been wholly one of bedevilment and frustration. For from the new celadon effect, originally unwanted, a new series of experiments was started, finally producing KCC#3, one of the best of my Koryo-type (as well as Ko-type) glazes detailed in Chapter 3. Thus, despite the still as yet unsolved conundrum of the earlier blue-spotted glaze, the search led in the direction of other fine glazes which without the prodding of frustration would never have been created. Robert Browning's suggestion that "a man's reach should exceed his grasp" is very close to the heart of the creative process. The best dividend of hard work is so often the one least expected.

And then, eight years later, after one more period of letting the whole question of the lost glaze lie fallow, a new look at the puzzle raised a possibility that really should have been considered much earlier. It was the possibility of my having made a productive *error*: perhaps the simplest of blunders, say, in weighing out the ingredients of the original glaze batch. Quickly, this line of investigation led in the direction of the kind of weighing mistake which would be most likely to affect the *color*, rather than the balance and texture characteristics of the glaze. Perhaps I had simply added *more* Fe_2O_3, in this case, yellow ochre, than my written calculations had specified! Instead of the called-for 2.5%, I had more likely weighed out something nearer to 12.5%, an easy enough error to make on a sliding-balance scale.

And so it was. Experiment soon established the ideal proportion of yellow ochre needed. In a few more firings I had recaptured the beautiful glaze with the cerulaean blue oil spots!

I append here, now, this most unusual glaze in its rediscovered formulation. It will be observed that its recipe is almost identical with its cognate celadon, KCC#3, but with two very important differences: the additional yellow ochre and the substitution of Maine feldspar for the Buckingham feldspar.

Batch Recipe	Maine feldspar	66.
	Georgia kaolin	4.
	Whiting	8.
	Flint	12.
	Softwood ash	10.
		100.
	Yellow ochre (10.5% of batch)	10.5

Procedures for KCC+Y2. Follow the directions for mixing, applying, drying, and firing given in Chapter 1. This glaze should be *dry*-milled about three-quarters of an hour at most; it can thus be kept indefinitely until needed for application.

The application itself should be quite thick; otherwise, no blue spots will form in the glaze. The usual caution must be taken to prevent over-wetting. In addition, because of the necessarily thick application and the tendency of the glaze to flow in heavy, viscous rolls toward the bottom of the ware, an unglazed area should be left on the lower, outer two inches of each piece, just as with a temmoku or an oxblood glaze. A wash of black iron oxide in water should first be applied to that area to harmonize with the glaze that will later flow down to and overlap it.

Note: A couple of extra cautionary notes are most necessary in connection with the handling of this glaze. (1) The efficacy of the iron diminishes while the glaze is kept in the wet state over long periods of time. Owing to bacterial action, a kind of biochemical degrading of both the iron oxide and the phosphorus apparently takes place. This fact (whatever the exact, scientific processes involved may be) would seem to explain the gradual transition of the aging glaze batch from one that produced a dark brown matrix with bright blue spots into one that could create only a dark green celadon that had just the faintest suggestion of a blue tinge. Obviously, therefore, to insure the appearance of the blue spots, it would be wise to make up a fresh batch of wet glaze for each firing. This caution is applicable to a good number of other glazes. As stated earlier in these pages, other glazes that definitely should be made up fresh each time are: the CR glazes, the CIH, CIW, and CIZ glazes, as well as COX#1 and CH+CX. Your experience will no doubt add others to the list. (2) *Of prime importance*: KCC+Y2 must *not* be applied to a body that is too high in silica. Dunting in big spirals throughout the piece is practically certain, either at once or weeks later, on such clay compositions as my Stoneware Body#4. On the other hand, the glaze makes a perfect fit with such formulations as my Stoneware Body #8. (The recipes for these are to be found in Chapter 11.) It is interesting that the silica is only 2% less in Body #8 than in Body #4, but it is significantly less to work very well with KCC+Y2.

Unexpected Troubles with KCC#3: Faulty Milling

It is an almost amusing irony (after the event) that even the fine Koryo-type celadon, KCC#3, which was only first discovered during my efforts to recapture KCC+Y2, also gave me a merry chase quite suddenly a few years later. The special caution I give in the procedure for KCC#3 about milling for one-half to three-quarters of an hour at the very most is the result of my own protracted and sad experiences. Suddenly, instead of the original, soft lovely glaze I had come to take almost for granted, batch after batch, firing after firing of the same glaze were now producing an ugly, lumpy, frothy mess. The problem was infuriating. It took me a long time, and many futile efforts in the pursuit of other theoretical possibilities, to discover the true cause of the trouble. Merely *over*milling KCC#3 had destroyed it! What a simple matter to correct, once it had been pinpointed. But its very simplicity had made it all the harder to detect.

New Possibilities from Varied Sources

I have detailed the frustrations and implied the delights of my search for "lost" glazes in the hope that it will inspire and encourage similar productive leaps into the dark by other potters. The joy of creation is both humanized and enriched by such challenges. In the effort to make a superb glaze, any approach is worth the trial; it can either teach us new humility or capture for us a new vision of elusive beauty. Both experiences are invaluable.

Thus, the ceramic artist who is deeply concerned with glazes must be constantly alert to new possibilities, and they are of so many different kinds! For example, as many of the glazes already explained plainly indicate, *very* slight changes in proportion of the same glaze components will often result in significant differences of color and texture. Then, too, the practice I explained in the previous chapter of overlapping one glaze with another not only produces interesting ceramic pieces in themselves, but it is strongly conducive to the inspired creation of new glazes.

The most direct suggestions for these possibilities are the result of simply applying one glaze over another; that result, when seen on a fired piece, often invites the experimenting potter to try formulating *as a new glaze* some combination of the two parent glazes. Even more exciting as possibilities, because they are at first inconspicuous—mere nuances—are the color, density, and texture of the *edge* of one glaze where it verges on and partly overlaps another, very different glaze on the same piece. The outcomes of such observations and the ensuing experimentation are often quite different from those that are inspired by the appearance of one glaze fully covering another.

Finally, and just as important as the foregoing, there is the urge to try out raw materials that are not customarily carried by ceramic supply houses. I have already instanced experiments with such substances as granite powder and red slate. Three or four more might well be added here to underscore the point that all of Nature seems to invite us to see what we can do (reverentially, it is to be hoped) with her bounty.

Celadons from Found Minerals

On one occasion, when I was visiting the site of an old abandoned New England iron mine deep in the hills, I picked up, just for their pistachio green beauty, some interesting specimens of epidote. Later, as I admired the lovely crystalline surfaces of some of the fragments, a possible connection with glazes (celadons?) suggested itself. Verification of the chemical composition of epidote—$Ca_2(Al, Fe)_3(SiO_4)_3(OH)$—further advanced the idea. I then obtained an average percentage analysis of this hydrous calcium iron silicate: 23.5% CaO, 11.5% Fe_2O_3, 25.0% Al_2O_3, 38.0% SiO_2, and less than 2% H_2O. Next came the application of the empirical theory of glaze calculation to this new material, using as my guide what I already knew about other celadon glazes. Soon I had made up several formulas and had then weighed out and milled batches of what might prove to be good celadons-with-a-difference. And so it turned out. Two of the best are given below. Both mature and require full reduction at cone 10, and are prepared and applied in the manner described in Chapters 1 and 3.

EP#2

This glaze offers an interesting range of effects, going from a clear, bright, celadon green in the outer areas (of bowl-shaped wares in particular) to a frosted, greenish matte in the center areas.

Empirical Formula	.0785 K_2O	.3497 Al_2O_3	3.115 SiO_2
	.7824 CaO	.0207 Fe_2O_3	
	.1391 Na_2O		

Batch Recipe	Epidote powder (50 mesh)	27.85
	Whiting	66.54
	Maine feldspar	157.0
	Georgia kaolin	6.37
	Flint	58.488
		316.248

EP#4

Quite different from the dual effects manifested in the previous glaze, EP#4 fires to a water-green celadon enriched by tiny, entrapped bubbles. In general appearance, it would seem to belong to the Lung-ch'üan family of glazes.

Empirical Formula	.08 K_2O	.4944 Al_2O_3	2.967 SiO_2
	.616 CaO	.0207 Fe_2O_3	
	.304 Na_2O		

Batch Recipe	Epidote powder (50 mesh)	27.85
	Whiting	49.9
	Nepheline syenite	177.4
	Flint	60.0
		315.15

Temmoku from Found Secondary Clays

Other backwoods rambles have yielded still other materials that are common enough and seem to demand experimental use. For example, from among three or four clay banks I have sampled, one, at least, has provided the basis for a valid glaze of a very individual sort. As might be expected, secondary clays tend to work well in the direction of temmokus; this one was most productive. The glaze I give below is singular in that it combines some of the best features of a hare's fur with those of a microcrystalline matte. Once again, the variation in one glaze is most observable when the glaze is fired on a bowl form; but, interestingly, it takes a reverse pattern from that seen in EP#2. Nearer the *outer* edges, the glaze has a soft matte texture and a light tan color; then, as this matte moves down toward the center of the bowl, it begins to break up into lustrous, dark brown streaks, and finally into hare's fur patterns. The glaze is best fired to cone 10 with full reduction, though it is also productive at lower work-heats. All procedures are the same as for the other temmokus described in Chapter 7.

Batch Recipe:	Local red clay	40.
T#24WR	Georgia kaolin	2.

Maine feldspar	33.
Whiting	25.
	100.
Red iron oxide (5% of batch)	5.

Temmoku from Traprock

The next illustration brings us back, literally, to bedrock. It is basalt, often referred to as "traprock." A bag of it was given to me by a generous friend, who also happens to be a highway supervisor, when I expressed some curiosity about its possibilities. After several tries, I came up with the following yellow-streaked temmoku, often red-brown matte near the lips of ware.

TR#9

This glaze is best fired to no more than cone 8 or 9 in full reduction. In a cone 10 firing, therefore, it would do best on the floor of the kiln. The procedures involved are precisely the same as those described in Chapter 7.

Batch Recipe		
	Flint	14.
	Georgia kaolin	10.
	Traprock (50 mesh)	33.
	Maine feldspar	27.
	Whiting	16.
		100.
	Red iron oxide (7% of batch)	7.

Preparatory Work Needed with Found Materials

It should be added in connection with crude materials like traprock, epidote, and secondary clays, that a certain amount of rough work in preparation of the substance is essential. Dug clays must first be dried, then pounded into dust, and finally sifted. Minerals will need more energetic pounding (often with sledge hammers) and more careful sifting. Initially, an ordinary kitchen sieve will serve for sifting in both cases; the last step requires a 50-mesh screen, at least. For the minerals, dry-milling in a ball mill will also help reduce small fragments to still smaller granules that can be incorporated into a glaze.

Some Inevitable Questions and Their Answers

Before leaving the subject of raw materials, I believe I should anticipate possible objections from some of my readers who may feel a sense of timidity or frustration at the idea of duplicating my work along these lines. Where, they may ask, are they to obtain such materials as granite powder, red slate, secondary clays, and wood ash? Obviously, not from the commercial supply houses. But is it not possible, they may persist, that commercially available substitutions can be worked into many of the celadons, Chüns, and temmokus described in this book, in place of the "natural" raw materials I indicate? The answer must be a qualified one: recent research has made laudable efforts to create subsitutions for such natural materials as wood ash with purified, commercially available substances. Such "synthetic" materials are at least worthy of experimental use; in fact, some of my own substitutions for wood ash have yielded quite promising results. (For further comment on wood ash subsitutions, together with "synthetic" wood ash formulas which I have worked out and experimented with, see Chapter 13.) I should hesitate to become so enthusiastic, however, as to equate the latter, quality for quality, in terms of color, texture, and depth, with the original glazes already detailed in these pages.

In the past, some of the apparent reasons for this discrepancy between more or less "natural" glazes and those made from purified substances have frequently been noted by such authorities as Hetherington and Leach. Purified materials are unfortunately just that: purified. Each contains little or nothing of the trace "impurities" that lend so much character to a glaze, particularly a Chinese Sung stoneware glaze. And deliberate attempts to introduce these impurities into a glaze mixture too often produce a rather artificial look, instead of the naturalness desired. Furthermore, those chemical elements and compounds that are so intimately bound together in the natural state of raw materials often cannot be introduced into a glaze in the same intricate form nor in just the proportions needed in any other way than the "natural" one. (Phosphorus especially is a case in point, and as we have noted, it is indispensable, not only to Chün, but also to a great many other Sung glazes.) And, finally, it is a fact that two glazes of the same theoretical chemical composition, but using different raw materials, often produce quite different results.

All of which brings us back to the first question asked: where to obtain these natural raw materials? There are two parts to the answer. First, as I have already remarked, what I have done any competent and dedicated potter can also do: he can obtain wood ash, for example, as I have, simply by carefully burning the necessary wood or by getting the ash from the waste fires of small lumber mills scattered through the countryside; he can obtain granite powder and traprock, or materials similar to them, by seeking out various granite and traprock sites; he can locate slate deposits and outcroppings, and pound and sift some of the scraps that litter these areas; he can dig into every clay bank he hears of. The other part of the answer is implicit in the first and has already been made obvious by everything said in this book, and particularly in this chapter: he can experiment. For example, using my work as his guide, if he so wishes, he can make analogous trials along the lines of my formulas with similar materials (other granites, rocks, clays, etc.) which he finds more easily obtainable. In fact, it is this same adventuresome spirit based on past achievement that I above all hope to encourage.

Dubious Experiments and Other Off-Chances

In further illustration, let us say I have been mulling over certain new possibilities for variations on old themes. For example, there is the newly discovered clay bank from which I have just obtained samples. What sort of new temmoku, if any, will it perhaps help create? As it turns out, the new clay material has such very strong fluxing qualities that it causes the glaze to flow too freely to create either good hare's fur lines or oil spots. It does produce a very clear, dark brown glaze with good depth; but though this quality is attractive enough, it isn't anything I strongly feel a need for. In any case, I haven't yet come up with the glaze formulation that will make this material yield any particularly desired effects to my satisfaction. I may put it aside for a time, then, until new experiences or insights give me the urge to try working with it again.

Or, more typically, I begin to see in a new light certain characteristics of an old glaze that I set aside many years ago as not quite satisfactory. It is a bluish celadon that contained an excess of wood ash and as a result developed a kind of dense opacity that seemed a bit dull to me then. On reexamining some fired examples of it, I now note with new interest both its extra viscosity and the faint streaks formed in the glaze as it slowly moved down the sides of the fired ware. Why not try to incorporate this characteristic into some of my temmoku glazes to produce a different, perhaps more authentic type of streak pattern in them for the hare's fur effect? In the past, I have already incorporated wood ash in some temmoku glazes, like T+CA72, but the quantity used was more or less sparing and served essentially to increase the fluxing power of the glaze. The thought now occurs to me, therefore, that an *excess* of wood ash in a glaze like T+CA72 might produce more viscosity, instead of less, together with partial devitrification of the glaze in lighter-colored, streaked patterns. And then again, it may not. This venture, as might be expected, draws a blank, or worse! For the excess of wood ash merely produces a very dull, crystalline gunmetal effect, instead of the hare's fur. But no matter what the result — and this is the point — something useful will have been learned from the experiment that possibly might be applied later to an entirely different set of glaze circumstances.

Another, quite divergent thought that also beckons is the off-chance of expanding the usefulness of some of my turquoise glazes, like AT#18, presented in Chapter 6. For example, there is the possibility that these high-sodium, low-alumina compositions may work well, not only with copper for the turquoise effect, but also with manganese to produce aubergine. Then, too, there is the idea of trying AT#18 just as it is, but with less copper, as a basis for local reduction red, using silicon carbide as the reducing agent. Or, going straight to the regular reducing fire in my gas kiln, I might try AT#18, again with less copper, but with an appropriate addition of tin oxide, as a proper reduction red. I reserve the actual testing of all these surmises for some future opportunity.

Promising Work with Volcanic Ash

One definitely successful recent experiment I have made has been with volcanic ash, a material, incidentally, that may be purchased from ceramic supply houses. I had already done some very promising work with various earths and sands, some of them volcanic, that I had picked up in my travels in different parts of the country. Used as partial substitutions in some of my older glaze formulations, for example, these new materials yielded interesting new color and textural qualities.

So it was, then, that when recently reordering basic supplies like feldspar and kaolin, I noticed the listing of volcanic ash, and decided to try some in the same way I had tried these various sands. A little study of representative analyses of volcanic ash revealed that it could fit neatly into a glaze formulation as a partial replacement for both feldspar and flint. It also has a relatively high iron content. It seemed very probable, therefore, that volcanic ash would be a suitable component in some such feldspathic formulation as my Chün glaze, CIH-p. And that is exactly what it was. As a start in that direction, I here append two excellent volcanic ash glaze variants of my light blue Chün that are effective in reduction firings at cones 9 and 10. They are prepared and handled in exactly the same ways as my regular CIH-p. (See Chapter 1.)

CIHp-Vol#1

This composition uses the volcanic ash as a generous substitution for the major portion of the feldspar and a sizable one of the flint, as well. More precisely, it makes up for about 70% of the feldspar and about 30% of the flint used in the original CIH-p glaze. The fired result is a darker, more intense, light blue Chün, capable of very luminous, still darker passages where touched by the flames.

Batch Recipe		
	Buckingham feldspar	16.
	Volcanic ash	47.
	Flint	15.
	Whiting	13.
	Softwood ash	9.
		100.
	Yellow ochre (2.5% of batch)	2.5

CIHp-Vol#2

Here the substitutions made by the volcanic ash have been cut in half. The result, as expected, is a much lighter blue Chün, but still quite different from the even lighter-hued, parent CIH-p glaze.

Batch Recipe		
	Buckingham feldspar	36.
	Volcanic ash	24.
	Flint	18.
	Whiting	13.
	Softwood ash	9.
		100.
	Yellow ochre (2.5% of batch)	2.5

In Conclusion

Thus, each time I come across a new material or develop a new glaze formulation, it seems an invitation to reexamine some of the older glazes for new light on possible changes and variations that may produce yet other new surfaces, colors, and textures. Obviously, then, there is nothing definitive and ultimate about my findings even after all my many years of research. Hopefully, the process of refinement upon refinement and new discovery will continue into the indefinite future. But I am also confident that anyone who is competent to use my present findings may, if he wishes, count on them as trustworthy points of departure for accomplishments of which he need not be ashamed. I assume that he, too, will transmit to others the best of which he is capable. Thus there may be a reassertion and a continuity of fine values in a truly fine art.

11
STONEWARE BODIES, SLIPS, STAINS, AND UNDERGLAZE

I have reserved for this and the succeeding chapters a number of supplementary kinds of information which, though quite important, might have bulked too large as interruptions in the earlier portions of the book. In this chapter, then, you will find the stoneware bodies on which the foregoing glazes have been fired, together with such related matters as slips, stains, and black underglaze.

Jordan Stoneware Bodies

One buff stoneware body I frequently use for many of the glazes I have described is Stoneware Body #4. It is excellent for throwing and stands up very well at cone 10. In oxidation it is a whitish buff; in full reduction it is a soft gray. In recent years, however, as the characteristics of such materials as Jordan clay have begun to change, the heaviest reduction of this body produces a much darker, browner coloration.

My other favorite clay composition, Stoneware Body #8, was first devised to prevent dunting and shivering with certain glazes. I use it with C1+G6F1, the second dark blue-and-brown mottled iron glaze in Chapter 4; the oil spot and deep black temmoku glazes given in Chapter 7; and, as explained in Chapter 10, the blue-spotted, dark brown glaze, KCC+Y2.

It is noteworthy that the adjustments between the Jordan clay and the flint, though slight, make a great difference. In fact, Stoneware Body #8 has worked so well with a wide spectrum of different glazes that it is perhaps preferable to Body #4 as an all-purpose stoneware clay.

Recipe for Stoneware Body #4	Jordan clay	53
	Ball clay	22
	Buckingham feldspar	5
	Flint	20
		100

Recipe for Stoneware Body #8	Jordan clay	55
	Ball clay	22
	Buckingham feldspar	5
	Flint	18
		100

Red Stoneware Bodies

The remaining stoneware bodies are red in oxidation and dark brown to almost black in reduction. Reduced, they are especially effective with temmoku, with Chün and Kuan-Chün, and with the dark blue-and-brown iron glazes. They frequently abet the oil spot effect and have a warming influence on the color of Chün and Kuan-Chün, In the case of G+CA1F1, these bodies intensify the background color of the glaze from its usual brown to deeper black and midnight blue. There are some drawbacks to their use, however. Though they throw rather well — but not as well as the other two bodies — they cannot stand up to the strains of cone 10 quite so ruggedly; that is, they are more easily warped, and especially in large, open pots that are horizontally extended, they have a slight tendency to slump. It is therefore advisable for cone 10 firings to use these red bodies mainly for bottles and vases, as well as for small or medium-sized bowls, preferably with wider feet.

The first of these red bodies I include here both as a matter of record, and more importantly, as a basis for the possible creation of similar bodies in the future. Despite its shortcomings, Stoneware Body #3 had long been a part of my standard potting procedure until just a few years ago when the supply of its chief component, Dalton #93 red clay, ran out and disappeared from the ceramic materials market. Though it did help produce the beautiful color effects described above, it at times had one additional disadvantage that spurred me on to try new formulations; this disadvantage was an occasional tendency to develop in the *body* and under the glaze rather large lumps or bubbles that probably consisted of entrapped carbon. This phenomenon occurred only under heavy reduction, and then not always. I attribute it to carbonaceous materials in the *fire clay* used. The body recipe is, as you see below, quite uncomplicated.

Recipe for Stoneware Body #3	Dalton #93 red clay	70
	Ball clay	18
	Fire clay (sifted)	12
		100

The red stoneware body I now use is not quite so rich a red as Body #3, but it totally avoids even the occasional occurrence of carbon bloat by dispensing with the fire clay and its impurities. At the same time, it works well with most of the same glazes and is less subject to warping or slumping at cone 10. The red clay it contains (available from the Cedar Heights Clay Co. of Oak Hill, Ohio) has the virtue of bringing the red color of the body to a fair approximation of Stoneware Body #3. It is possible that higher proportions of the Cedar Heights clay than I now use would improve the color without adding to the danger of warping and slumping.

Recipe for Stoneware Body #17	Jordan clay	32
	Cedar Heights Redart clay	25
	Ball clay	18
	Buckingham feldspar	5
	Flint	20
		100

White Slips

As for slips, it is the white ones that best harmonize with the kinds of glazes I have described. They are particularly helpful with such glazes as oxblood and turquoise, and of course are indispensable for certain Tz'u-chou effects. As previously indicated, these white slips are best applied to the leatherhard ware when the latter is not *too* dry, and then are bisqued with it. The best method of application for a smooth, uniform surface is spraying; the use of a broad, flat brush, on the other hand, will often produce interesting variations in tone under the glaze. The best of these white slips follow.

Recipe for White Slip #6	Flint	34
	Cornwall stone	30
	Georgia kaolin	25
	Ball clay	10
	Soda ash	1
		100

Recipe for White Slip #9	Flint	40.6
	Maine feldspar	20.1
	Georgia kaolin	28.3
	Ball clay	10.0
	Soda ash	1.0
		100.0

Stains

Another surface treatment, especially of bisqued, as yet unglazed ware, is the use of simple oxide washes or stains applied with a broad, flat brush. Mention has already been made of black iron oxide mixed with water as a coating under some temmoku glazes. By itself, without any glaze, black iron oxide burns to an interesting dark brown sheen in cone 10 reduction firings. Thus, a suitably darkened surface that harmonizes with the glaze covering the rest of the piece can be achieved; this quality is especially desirable for the unglazed lower portions of a temmoku bowl, for example. An aqueous mix of yellow ochre also makes a fine surface dressing, and under certain glazes (e.g., of the Bristol type) will promote interesting special glaze effects. As already remarked, it can also be used as an *on*-glaze decoration, either by itself, or as part of a palette of other common oxides like cobalt and red iron, as well as with underglaze mixtures.

Underglaze Black

Frequent mention has also been made in these pages of underglaze black for brush-work, both under and over the glazes themselves. One of my best compositions for this purpose is given below. In preparing it, I advise that small quantities of this mixture be wet-ground in a mortar and pestle. The best method of grinding in this case is to fasten the mortar with wads of clay to the throwing head of a kick wheel, and to kick the wheel slowly to aid the rotation of the pestle within the mortar. For painting decorations, the ideal tool is a Chinese brush. Handling of the underglaze black can be facilitated by adding a few drops of either corn syrup or gum tragacanth to the mixture to smooth it out.

Recipe for Underglaze Black #3		
	Black ferrous oxide	43
	Manganese oxide	18
	Cobalt oxide	15
	Nickel oxide	15
	Chromium oxide	9
		100

12
GLAZE
CALCULATION

In this chapter, I offer the reader something he may have hitherto shied away from because it seemed either too difficult or of doubtful value. My experience has shown that it is neither.

Though there are comprehensive treatments of the empirical theory of glaze calculation in the works of Parmelee and Andrews, for example, the following explanations of how I have applied this theory to my creation of certain glazes may prove valuable to the interested potter. And if he will patiently follow each step, without hurrying ahead of himself, the process will not really be so difficult after all.

Method I: From Chemical Analysis to Batch Recipe

A serviceable example to start with is the parent of my ACG group of glazes. The calculations that went into its development follow:

1. As already explained in an earlier chapter, I began my work on ACG with the chemical analysis of an "ancient Chinese glaze" made by H. W. Nichols as reported by Parmelee. That analysis was given in percentages as:

Silica	54.17%
Alumina	14.16%
Ferric oxide	4.38%
Lime	19.05%
Magnesia	2.04%
Alkalies	5.49%
	99.29%

The total of 99.29% implies the possible existence (besides H_2O) of trace minerals, such as phosphorus, which must have lent "character" to the original glaze. However, on this occasion, choosing to adhere strictly to the empirical theory approach, I dispensed with the attempt to incorporate into the reconstituted glaze such materials as wood ash, and relied solely on the standard, commercially available substances. For similar reasons of simplification, I assumed the "alkalies" mentioned to be solely potassium oxide. Thus, the basic chemical analysis and the initial observations made of that analysis represent the first step.

2. The next step taken toward arriving at an empirical formula was to *divide* the percentage of each of the chemical compounds listed by its *molecular weight*. The molecular weight of a compound is the sum of the weights of its atomic parts. For example, in the case of SiO_2 (silica or flint), silicon has an atomic weight of 28.06, and oxygen has a weight of 16.00; thus, Si taken once equals 28.06, and oxygen taken twice equals 32.00, the combined result or molecular weight being 60.06, or more simply, 60. (To obviate this part of the computations, there are comprehensive charts of chemical constants for ceramic raw materials available, such as the one printed in Parmelee. Later in this chapter I have included a briefer table that answers most of the needs of stoneware glaze calculation.) The rest of the listing of molecular weights follows the same procedure. Thus we have our percentages divided by their respective molecular weights as follows:

Compounds	Percentages		Molecular Weights		Equivalents
Silica (SiO_2)	54.17	÷	60	=	0.902
Alumina (Al_2O_3)	14.16	÷	102	=	0.138
Ferric oxide (Fe_2O_3)	4.38	÷	160	=	0.027
Lime (CaO)	19.05	÷	56	=	0.340
Magnesia (MgO)	2.04	÷	40	=	0.051
Potassium oxide (K_2O)	5.49	÷	94	=	0.058

3. Next I isolated, for computation purposes, the *monoxide* group in the list of equivalents. In ceramic calculation, this group is usually designated the *RO* group, whereas the other compounds fall into two other groups: R_2O_3 (the sesquioxides, as in the case of Al_2O_3 Fe_2O_3, or B_2O_3); and RO_2 (dioxides such as SiO_2). These groupings attempt to clarify the balances in a glaze, between the alkalies and bases (RO) and the acids (RO_2), with the R_2O_3 group acting as an intermediate, since Al_2O_3, for example, acts as both an acid and a base. Coming back to our illustration, we thus have the following rearrangement of the equivalents under the three different oxide headings:

RO	R_2O_3	RO_2
.340 CaO	.138 Al_2O_3	.902 SiO_2
.051 MgO	.027 Fe_2O_3	
.058 K_2O		
.449		

4. We then take the total of the RO equivalents, or .449, and using it as a factor divide it into each of the equivalents in all groups. In the case of the RO group, it converts that group to unity, or approximately the total of 1.0000. The result is the empirical formula. (As pointed out by Ralph J. Cook in his special article included in Parmelee,

"An empirical formula is the same as a molecular formula except that it does not represent a molecule," neither the glaze nor its components being "a true molecular compound."):

$$.7572 \text{ CaO} \qquad .3073 \text{ Al}_2\text{O}_3 \qquad 2.2316 \text{ SiO}_2$$
$$.1135 \text{ MgO} \qquad .0601 \text{ Fe}_2\text{O}_3$$
$$\underline{.1291 \text{ K}_2\text{O}}$$
$$.9998$$

5. We are now ready to convert this empirical formula into the batch weights of the raw materials most commonly used to supply the necessary oxides. Some raw materials supply just the *one* oxide needed, as, for example, in the case of whiting, which is a standard source of CaO. Other raw materials contribute to two or more oxides, as is true in the case of kaolin, which provides one part of Al_2O_3 to every two parts of SiO_2. Buckingham feldspar contributes to three oxides in the following proportions: 1 part of K_2O; 1.13 parts of Al_2O_3; 6.45 parts of SiO_2. These facts are taken into account in the following computations, in which, for ease in handling, the oxides in the empirical formula are arranged as headings:

Empirical Formula

CaO	MgO	K$_2$O	Al$_2$O$_3$	Fe$_2$O$_3$	SiO$_2$	Molecular Equivalents	Raw Materials
.7572	.1135	.1291	.3075	.0601	2.2316		
.7572						.7572	Whiting
x							
	.1135					.1135	Magnesium carbonate
	x						
		.1291	.1458		.8326	.1291	Buckingham feldspar
		x	.1615		1.3990		
			.1615		.3230	.1615	Kaolin
			x		1.076		
					1.076	1.076	Flint
					x		
				.0601		.0601	Red iron oxide
				x			

For further clarification of the above example: (1) The molecular equivalents contributed by each raw material (e.g., .7572 of whiting) are *subtracted* from those equivalent headings in the empirical formula (e.g., .7572 CaO) to which each contributes. (2) *Before* subtracting, the molecular equivalent of a *complex* raw material like Buckingham feldspar should be *multiplied* by the amount (proportion) of each of its separate components. Thus, .1291 of Buckingham feldspar is multiplied by 1 to indicate the amount of K_2O it brings to the glaze; .1291 is also multiplied by 1.13 for the Al_2O_3 it supplies; and .1291 is finally multiplied by 6.45 for the SiO_2. The results, then, are: .1291 of K_2O; .1458 of Al_2O_3; and .8326 of SiO_2. These, in turn, are *subtracted* from the .1291 K_2O, the .3070 Al_2O_3, and the 2.2316 SiO_2, respectively, of the empirical formula. (3) In the same way, the *remainders* of these subtractions are either wholly or partially supplied by the next raw material, kaolin. This material wholly supplies the .1615 of Al_2O_3 and at the same time, therefore, supplies 2 times .1615 of SiO_2, or .3230 of SiO_2. (4) The other, simpler raw materials wholly supply all the other remaining equivalents called for by the empirical formula (and nothing else besides that need be calculated).

Note: There are some exceptions to this procedure, however. These occur when the monoxide group in a raw material is in a higher proportion than 1.0 to the rest of its composition (i.e., not yet in unity). A typical example of such a raw material is colemanite, the chemical composition of which, in ceramic terms, is: $2CaO, 3B_2O_3$. The reader is advised to consult *Notes on Calculations with Certain Materials* later in this chapter for the special method used in calculating such materials into a glaze formula.

6. The final step in arriving at the batch recipe is to *multiply* each of the raw material equivalents by the molecular equivalent weight of that raw material. (This molecular equivalent weight is arrived at either by simply consulting the chart included later in this chapter or, much more laboriously, by adding up the component atomic weights of the oxides contained in the raw material. Thus, Buckingham feldspar, the formula of which is K_2O, 1.13 Al_2O_3, 6.45 SiO_2, contains, in atomic weight, 94 of K_2O, 115 of Al_2O_3, and 387 of SiO_2 — or a total of 596, its molecular equivalent weight.) To obtain the batch weight, this final calculation follows:

Raw Materials	Molecular Equivalents		Molecular Equivalent Weights		Batch Weights
Whiting	.7572	X	100	=	75.72
Magnesium carbonate	.1135	X	84	=	9.53
Buckingham feldspar	.1291	X	596	=	76.94
Kaolin	.1615	X	258	=	41.66
Flint	1.076	X	60	=	64.56
Red iron oxide	.061	X	160	=	9.61

Thus, I arrived at the final step for my ACG glaze, the batch weights being the same as the batch recipe for the glaze.

The batch recipe may then be weighed out in grams, in ounces, or in any other convenient unit of measurement, and the combined materials at last thoroughly mixed (as described in earlier chapters) with sufficient water to make the glaze ready for application to the ware. As for the particular glaze I have just finished calculating from percentage chemical analysis to final batch recipe, I call it the "parent" of my ACG group of glazes because, not being fully satisfied with the first fired results, I soon created variations of it that answered my expectations more completely. One of these variations will serve as illustrative material in the next section of this chapter.

Method II: The Usual, Shorter Approach from Empirical Formula to Batch Recipe

ACGW-H4 is particularly worth examining here, first because of the extent to which it differs from ACG and, second, because it exemplifies the comparative ease with which most glaze calculations can usually be done. Most of the time the potter will not be starting his calculations with percentage chemical analysis, but instead with an empirical formula, the latter being (as we have seen) several stages nearer the end of the whole process. Such a procedure normally involves only three steps, essentially corresponding to the final three steps of Method I:

1. Here we begin with the assumed empirical formula of ACGW-H4:

$$.7572 \; CaO \qquad .375 \; Al_2O_3 \qquad 2.85 \; SiO_2$$
$$.1135 \; MgO$$
$$.1291 \; K_2O$$

It will be observed that the RO group is identical with that of ACG itself. However, the Al_2O_3 represents an increase of .0677, and the SiO_2 an increase of .6184 over these respective oxides in the ACG empirical. The outcome in the fired result in this case is actually a *lowered* eutectic point, in other words, a lower temperature at which the mixture of constituents will fuse and melt.

2. The molecular equivalents for the raw materials to be used in ACGW-H4 are then computed as follows (see Step 5 above in Method I for the detailed explanation of the arithmetical procedures involved here):

Empirical Formula					Molecular Equivalents	Raw Materials
CaO	MgO	K_2O	Al_2O_3	SiO_2		
.7572	.1135	.1291	.375	2.85		
.7572					.7572	Whiting
x						
	.1135				.1135	Magnesium carbonate
	x					
		.1291	.1458	.8326	.1291	Buckingham feldspar
		x	.2292	2.0174		
			.2292	.4584	.2292	Kaolin
			x	1.5590		
				1.559	1.559	Flint
				x		

3. Here we convert the molecular equivalents of the raw materials into the batch recipe for ACGW-H4. In other words, we *multiply* the raw materials equivalents by the molecular equivalent weight of each.

Raw Materials	Molecular Equivalents		Molecular Equivalent Weights		Batch Weights
Whiting	.7572	X	100	=	75.72
Magnesium carbonate	.1135	X	84	=	9.53
Buckingham feldspar	.1291	X	596	=	76.94
Kaolin	.2292	X	258	=	59.13
Flint	1.559	X	60	=	93.44
					314.76

You have probably observed that so far I have omitted the Fe_2O_3 from the picture. This was done, first, because the proportion in the parent ACG was much too large for my purpose, and, second, because the addition of colorant oxides to a glaze is simpler to calculate when done in the form of percentages of the total batch weight. Thus, when varying the above glaze to increase its usefulness as a Lung-ch'üan celadon, I found that the addition of 1% Fe_3O_4 (black iron oxide) to the total batch weight was the ideal proportion. Accordingly, for my ACGW4-F3 celadon I add 3.14 grams of black iron oxide to each 314.76 grams of the total weight of the batch recipe.

Method III: Incorporating "Natural" Materials into Glaze Calculations

Some illustration is in order to show how "natural" raw materials with a known percentage analysis, such as granite powder or epidote, can be adapted to the empirical theory of glaze calculation. For example, in simplified form, here is how the celadon I call G#6 was arrived at. (The method used is merely a combination, in continuous sequence, of Methods I and II. I therefore condense some of the steps and refer the reader back to the analogous procedures spelled out in those methods:

1. To begin with, I had a percentage chemical analysis of the granite powder from Barre, Vermont:

SiO_2	70.0 %
Al_2O_3	15.35%
CaO	2.0 %
Na_2O	5.2 %
K_2O	4.45%
Fe_2O_3	2.0 %
Loss on Ignition	1.0 %

2, 3, and 4. Using the successive procedures of dividing these percentages by their respective molecular weights, rearranging the resultant equivalents into the three RO groupings, and then reducing them to unity (as detailed above under Method I), I arrived at the *empirical formula* for this granite powder:

.2835 K_2O	.9016 Al_2O_3	6.9904 SiO_2
.214 CaO	.0749 Fe_2O_3	(.3329 H_2O)*
.5023 Na_2O		

*derived from the 1.07 L.O.I. (see table below and *Glossary*).

5. Brief mention has been made parenthetically under Method I of how to arrive at the molecular equivalent weight of a raw material. Here, for a new substance like granite powder, it would be wise to spell out for the reader the exact procedure in full detail.

To obtain the molecular weight of a "natural" raw material, we must add together the molecular weights of each of the oxides in its empirical formula. To achieve these individual molecular weights, each component is *first* multiplied by its own equivalent weight (as listed in the table later in this chapter). Thus, the molecular weight of .2835 K_2O is .2835 times 94, or 26.649. Similarly, .214 CaO times 56 equals 11.984, etc. When all the component oxides in the empirical formula have had their molecular equivalents multiplied by their respective equivalent weights, the results are added together and we thereby arrive at the molecular weight of the whole substance. In this case, the granite powder's molecular weight adds up to 599.34.

The following chart presents the whole computation:

Oxides	Molecular Equivalents		Molecular Weights		Weight Ratio
K_2O	.2835	X	94	=	26.649
CaO	.214	X	56	=	11.984
Na_2O	.5023	X	62	=	31.142
Al_2O_3	.9016	X	102	=	91.963
Fe_2O_3	.0749	X	160	=	12.184
SiO_2	6.9904	X	60	=	419.424
H_2O	.3329	X	18	=	5.992
Granite Powder Molecular Weight				=	599.338

6. It is useful to note that by itself this granite powder produces a rather dark brown glaze, quite viscous and matte at cone 8, and glossier and more fluid at cones 9 and 10. Taking these latter characteristics into account, I then tentatively assumed several feldspathic glazes that would logically accommodate the range of oxides found in the granite powder. One of the most successful, when finally reduction fired to cones 9 and 10, was G#6. The empirical formula I had assumed for G#6 was:

.0785 K_2O	.3497 Al_2O_3	4.115 SiO_2
.7824 CaO	.0207 Fe_2O_3	
.1391 Na_2O		

7. This is the computation required to arrive at the molecular equivalents of the raw materials to be used in making G#6:

Empirical Formula						Molecular Equivalents	Raw Materials
K_2O	CaO	Na_2O	Al_2O_3	Fe_2O_3	SiO_2		
.0785	.7824	.1391	.3497	.0207	4.115		
.0785	.0592	.1391	.2497	.0207	1.9374	.277	Granite powder
x	.7232	x	.1	x	2.1776		
	.7232					.7232	Whiting
	x						
			.1		.2	.1	Kaolin
			x		1.9776		
					1.9776	1.9776	Flint
					x		

8. Finally, we convert the molecular equivalents of the raw materials into the batch recipe for G#6:

Raw Materials	Molecular Equivalents		Molecular Equivalent Weights		Batch Weights
Granite powder	.277	X	599.34	=	166.01
Whiting	.7232	X	100.	=	72.32
Kaolin	.1	X	258.	=	25.8
Flint	1.9776	X	60.	=	118.65
					382.78

In the case of this celadon, as you may have observed, there is no necessity to add any more iron oxide as a colorant, since the granite powder itself yields just the right amount. In fact, part of the rationale for the choice of the particular empirical formula is obviously dictated by the empirical proportion of Fe_2O_3 wanted, at most .0207. Similarly, the proportions of K_2O (.0785) and Na_2O (.1391) were chosen not only to fit in with the fundamental limitations imposed by the .0207 of Fe_2O_3, but also by the desire to obviate the addition of any feldspathic material other than the granite powder itself. The batch weights thus become a very simple recipe with four ingredients.

9. **(optional)** In conclusion, I should point out, for those who prefer their batch recipes in the form of *percentages*, that one further computation will yield this arrangement. Simply, it consists of using the *total* of the batch weights to *divide* into the weight of *each component*. Thus, the total batch weight of G#6 being 382.78, the percentage composition of the glaze becomes:

Granite powder	43.3%
Whiting	18.9%
Kaolin	6.8%
Flint	31.0%
	100.0%

Material	Formula	Equivalent Weight
Albite	$Na_2O, Al_2O_3, 6SiO_2$	524
Alumina	Al_2O_3	102
Aluminum phosphate	Al, PO_4	122
Amblygonite	Li, AlF, PO_4	148
Barium carbonate	$BaCO_3$	197
Barium oxide	BaO	153
Bentonite	$Al_2O_3, 4SiO_2, 9H_2O$	504
Bone ash	$Ca_3(PO_4)_2$	103 (RO)
Borax	$Na_2O, 2B_2O_3, 10H_2O$	382
Calcium borate	$2CaO, 3B_2O_3, 5H_2O$	206 (RO)
Calcium oxide	CaO	56
Calcium phosphate	$Ca_3(PO_4)_2$	103 (RO)
China clay	$Al_2O_3, 2SiO_2, 2H_2O$	258
Chromium oxide	Cr_2O_3	152
Cobalt oxide (cobaltous)	CoO	75
Colemanite	$2CaO, 3B_2O_3, 5H_2O$	206 (RO)
Copper carbonate	$CuCO_3$	124
Copper oxide (cupric)	CuO	80
Dolomite	$CaCO_3, MgCO_3$	92 (RO)
Epidote	$Ca_2(Al,Fe)_3, (SiO_4)_3, (OH)$	238

Feldspathic Materials:

Material	Formula	Equivalent Weight
Buckingham feldspar	$K_2O, 1.13\,Al_2O_3, 6.45\,SiO_2$	596
Cornwall stone (typical)	$.63\,KNaO$ $\quad 1.3497\,Al_2O_3$ $.32\,CaO$ $\quad\quad .0181\,Fe_2O_3$ $.05\,MgO$ $\quad 10.1227\,SiO_2$	1550
Cornwall stone (theoretical)	$IRO, 2.5Al_2O_3, 20SiO_2$	1550
Granite powder (Barre)	$.2835\,K_2O$ $\quad .9016\,Al_2O_3$ $.214\,\;\,CaO$ $\quad .749\;\;Fe_2O_3$ $.5023\,Na_2O$ $\;6.9904\,SiO_2$	599
Kona F-4 feldspar	$.2649\,K_2O$ $\quad .9979\,Al_2O_3$ $.5770\,Na_2O$ $.1574\,CaO$ $\quad 5.7833\,SiO_2$	518

(table continued next page)

Material	Formula	Equivalent Weight
Maine sodium feldspar	$.64\ Na_2O$ } $1.18\ Al_2O_3$ $.36\ K_2O$ } $8.8\ \ SiO_2$	722
Nepheline syenite	$.25\ K_2O$ } $1.11\ Al_2O_3$ $.75\ Na_2O$ } $4.65\ SiO_2$	462
Orthoclase	$K_2O, Al_2O_3, 6SiO_2$	556
Ferric oxide	Fe_2O_3	160
Ferrous oxide	FeO	72
Ferroso-ferric oxide	Fe_3O_4	{ $155\ (R_2O_3)$ { $78\ (RO)$
Flint	SiO_2	60
Kaolin	$Al_2O_3, 2SiO_2, 2H_2O$	258
Lead carbonate (white)	$2PbCO_3, Pb(OH)_2$	258 (RO)
Lead oxide (litharge)	PbO	223
Lead oxide (red) (minium)	Pb_3O_4	228 (RO)
Lime (calcium oxide)	CaO	56
Lithium carbonate	Li_2CO_3	74
Magnesium carbonate	$MgCO_3$	84
Manganese carbonate	$MnCO_3$	115
Manganese dioxide (pyrolusite)	MnO_2	87
Nickel oxide (green)	NiO	75
Potassium oxide	K_2O	94
Silica	SiO_2	60
Sodium bicarbonate	$NaHCO_3$	168 (RO)
Sodium carbonate (crystal) (sal soda)	$Na_2CO_3, 10H_2O$	286
Sodium carbonate (fused) (soda ash)	Na_2CO_3	106
Sodium oxide	Na_2O	62
Sodium phosphate	$Na_2HPO_4, 10H_2O$	322 (RO)
Spodumene	$Li_2O, Al_2O_3, 4SiO_2$	372
Talc	$3MgO, 4SiO_2, H_2O$	378
Tin oxide (stannic)	SnO_2	151
Titanium oxide	TiO_2	80
Whiting	$CaCO_3$	100
Zinc oxide	ZnO	81
Zirconium oxide	ZrO_2	123

Element	Symbol	Atomic Weight	Element	Symbol	Atomic Weight
Aluminum	Al	26.97	Magnesium	Mg	24.32
Barium	Ba	137.36	Manganese	Mn	54.93
Boron	B	10.82	Nickel	Ni	58.69
Calcium	Ca	40.08	Oxygen	O	16.00
Carbon	C	12.01	Phosphorus	P	30.98
Chromium	Cr	52.01	Potassium	K	39.096
Cobalt	Co	58.94	Selenium	Se	78.96
Copper	Cu	63.54	Silicon	Si	28.06
Fluorine	F	19.00	Sodium	Na	22.997
Hydrogen	H	1.008	Tin	Sn	118.70
Iron	Fe	55.85	Titanium	Ti	47.90
Lead	Pb	207.21	Zinc	Zn	65.38
Lithium	Li	6.940	Zirconium	Zr	91.22

Notes on Calculations with Certain Raw Materials

It is necessary to remark on the method of incorporating into a typical glaze calculation certain of the ceramic raw materials listed in the *Table of Chemical Constants*. The need arises when the monoxides (RO) in a substance are in a higher proportion than 1 to the rest of the oxides involved (e.g. $2CaO, 3B_2O_3$). In order to obtain the desired fraction of one such material to be used in a formula, the following general principle is basic:

The molecular equivalent of a particular oxide *required* for the empirical formula *must be divided by* what is *present* of that particular oxide in the raw material. The result of this division will then be used as the factor (or molecular equivalent) for the raw material, and so may be used in calculating the actual amount of that material into the batch recipe.

To illustrate, let us examine the method of using colemanite in a glaze calculation. Colemanite's formula is $2CaO, 3B_2O_3$ with a molecular weight of 412. For calculating purposes, it is first necessary to reduce the CaO to unity. This means *dividing* the formula of colemanite *and* its equivalent weight *in half*. The result then becomes: $1CaO, 1.5B_2O_3$, with an equivalent weight of 206. Now, taking the B_2O_3 as the oxide for which the predetermined molecular equivalent is required in the empirical formula, we *divide* that molecular equivalent by the factor 1.5 (the proportion of B_2O_3 in the *unity* formula of colemanite) to give us the amount of colemanite that will contain the molecular equivalent of B_2O_3 needed in the empirical formula we are working on.

An illustration is indispensable to understanding the latter statement. Specifically, then, let us say that .375 molecular equivalents of B_2O_3 are needed in a particular empirical formula. The raw material, colemanite, would work out with this requirement as follows:

$$\frac{.375 \ B_2O_3 \ \text{(called for in the formula)}}{1.5 \ \ \ \ B_2O_3 \ \text{(present in the colemanite)}} = .25 \quad \left\{ \begin{array}{l} \text{the ``amount,'' or equivalent, of} \\ \text{colemanite that will provide} \\ .375 \ B_2O_3 \end{array} \right.$$

It next follows that the CaO equivalent supplied by this same amount of colemanite would be .25 (that is, 1CaO times .25). Any *additional* CaO needed in the predetermined empirical formula can, of course, be supplied by whiting. So, for example, if an empirical formula were to require, among other components, .6 of CaO and .375 of B_2O_3, the equivalent of .25 colemanite (as detailed above) would supply *all* the B_2O_3 needed (or .375), as well as *some* of the CaO needed to the extent of .25. The remaining .35 of CaO required could be supplied by .35 of whiting. In the final conversion into the batch recipe, the .25 colemanite factor is *multiplied* by the colemanite equivalent weight of 206, the result being 51.5. This last number represents the amount of actual colemanite (whether in grams, ounces, or pounds) to be weighed out in the batch recipe.

One more illustration will serve to underscore the method involved. The raw material I take for my example here is bone ash. The oxides of bone ash entering into fusion when fired are $3CaO,P_2O_5$, with a molecular weight of 310. Reduced to RO unity, the formula for this substance becomes $1CaO,.333P_2O_5$, with an equivalent weight of 103. Because the main purpose in using bone ash in a glaze is to introduce a required amount of phosphorus, we will use the molecular equivalent needed for P_2O_5 as the basis for our computation. Thus, if .02 of P_2O_5 is needed in a particular empirical formula, we have:

$$\frac{.02 \ \ \text{(the } P_2O_5 \ \text{needed in the formula)}}{.333 \ \text{(the } P_2O_5 \ \text{proportion in the bone ash)}} = .06 \quad \left\{ \begin{array}{l} \text{the ``amount,'' or equivalent, of} \\ \text{bone ash that will provide} \\ .02 \ \text{mol. equiv. of } P_2O_5 \end{array} \right.$$

This equivalent of .06, in turn, represents the portion of CaO that will be supplied by .06 equivalent of bone ash. Any additional CaO needed in the empirical formula can be supplied by whiting. Thus, the amount of P_2O_5 needed in the formula would be *entirely* supplied, and the CaO needed would be *partly* supplied, by a .06 equivalent of bone ash. In converting into the batch recipe, the .06 equivalent is multiplied by the bone ash equivalent weight of 103, the result being 6.18, which represents the amount of actual bone ash to be weighed out in the basic batch recipe.

13
SYNTHETIC WOOD ASH

Comment having been made in Chapter 10 on the idea of synthesizing substitutes for "natural" raw materials, I think it might be interesting and useful to the venturesome potter to experiment with a couple of such synthetics that I have worked out for wood ash. But before giving their composition, I believe it equally important to offer a brief account of the lines of investigation that accompanied my development of each of these synthetics.

First, I was struck by the discrepancies between the analyses of the same wood ash material as reported in two reputable sources. One is cited by Bernard Leach, in his *A Potter's Book*, as the result of exhaustive work done by J.B.E. Patterson at the Darlington Hall Laboratory; and the other is offered in a table of such analyses in Herbert Sanders' *The World of Japanese Ceramics*. The wood ash in question is "*issu*-wood ash," said to be a very popular wood ash for ceramics in Japan, and obtained from the *issu* or *Distylium racemosum* tree. The percentage analyses follow as printed in each source (Patterson's material being described as "fully washed," and Sanders' bearing no reference to washing, one way or another):

Issu-Wood Ash Oxides	Patterson Analysis	Sanders Analysis
SiO_2	71.96	34.60
Al_2O_3	0.63	4.38
P_2O_5	0.42	3.93
Fe_2O_3	0.28	0.49
CaO	15.95	47.71
K_2O	0.84	2.51
Na_2O	—	0.06
MgO	1.57	5.99
CO_3 (or L.O.I.)	8.29	—
	99.94	99.67

If the above table has any significance, it is simply that we are not dealing with anything resembling standardized materials when we refer to "wood ash," even of a *specific* type. (Either that, or only one of these two analyses happens to be correct, though both come from unimpeachable sources deserving serious consideration.)

This impression receives further support from the fact that my own synthetic substitute for "common" (or what I call, "mixed") ash bears only partial resemblance to the synthetic substitute worked out by Masatarō Ōnishi as reported in Sanders' book. For I had based my calculations squarely on the percentage analysis of "common ash" given in the same book, on the assumption that both the percentage analysis and Ōnishi's synthetic recipe derived from at least similar samples of this material. Retracing our steps, here is Sanders' percentage analysis of "common ash":

SiO_2	30.99
P_2O_5	1.91
Al_2O_3	8.91
Fe_2O_3	3.04
CaO	22.42
MgO	3.30
K_2O	3.91
Na_2O	2.33
MnO	1.26
L.O.I.	21.44

From this analysis, I worked out the following empirical formula:

"Common Ash"	.690 CaO	.150 Al_2O_3	.881 SiO_2
Empirical Formula	.142 MgO	.0327 Fe_2O_3	.025 P_2O_5
(Grebanier)	.071 K_2O		
	.064 Na_2O		
	.0305 MnO		

The batch recipe, worked out in terms of percentage proportions, followed:

Batch Recipe for Synthetic "Common Ash" (Grebanier)

Bone ash	4.09
Whiting	35.73
Magnesium carbonate	6.86
Buckingham feldspar	24.35
Kaolin	10.39
Flint	10.11
Soda ash	3.90
Managnese dioxide	1.32
Red iron oxide	3.00
	99.95

This contrasts strongly with the following:

Batch Recipe for Synthetic "Common Ash" (Maratarō Ōnishi)

Bone ash	7.0
Limestone	62.0 .
Magnesite	5.0
Fukishima feldspar	12.0
Korean kaolin	10.0
Silica	3.0
	99.0

The one constituent raw material in Ōnishi's recipe that has a fairly wide variation from materials commonly available in America is, of course, Fukishima feldspar. The percentage analysis of it given by Sanders shows that it is essentially a sodium feldspar with an empirical formula (as I worked it out from the percentage analysis given) of:

$$.553 \; K_2O \qquad .991 \; Al_2O_3 \qquad 5.736 \; SiO_2$$
$$.392 \; Na_2O \qquad .003 \; Fe_2O_3$$
$$.024 \; CaO$$
$$.030 \; MgO$$

Any attempt to apply this Fukishima feldspar empirical with nicety to parts of the empirical formula I derived for "common ash" does not, however, really work out. Not only does it fall short of supplying the proportion of Na_2O needed by the synthetic ash formula, but the balance between its Al_2O_3 and SiO_2 is such that it fills *most* of the SiO_2 needed in the synthetic ash formula and *not enough* of the Al_2O_3 needed. As a result of the latter fact, the addition of kaolin that must then follow would inevitably provide an *excess of* SiO_2, even without the 3% of silica added thereto in Maratarō Ōnishi's recipe. It is also obvious, at a glance, that his recipe leaves quite out of account the over 1% of manganese dioxide and the 3% of iron oxide which my recipe necessarily derives from the given percentage analysis of "common ash." Such omissions I consider especially serious, since at least part of the character of a *natural* wood ash glaze probably depends on sufficient amounts of such oxides, as well as on traces of other minerals.

Coupled with my development of a "common," or mixed-wood ash synthetic substitute was that of a synthetic *pine* ash. Using the percentage analysis of a natural pine ash given in Sanders' book as a starting point, I worked out a serviceable empirical formula and then a batch recipe for a *synthetic* pine ash. To begin with, the analysis of natural pine ash reported by Sanders is:

SiO_2	24.39
P_2O_5	2.78
Al_2O_3	9.71
Fe_2O_3	3.41

CaO	39.73
MgO	4.45
K$_2$O	8.98
Na$_2$O	3.77
MnO	2.74
	99.96

My derived empirical formula and batch recipe in percentage proportions follow:

Pine Ash Empirical Formula (Grebanier)

.6987 CaO	.0936 Al$_2$O$_3$	.4002 SiO$_2$
.1094 MgO	.0209 Fe$_2$O$_3$	.0192 P$_2$O$_5$
.0940 K$_2$O		
.0598 Na$_2$O		
.0379 MnO		

Batch Recipe for Synthetic Pine Ash (Grebanier)

Bone ash	4.10
Whiting	44.37
Magnesium carbonate	6.36
Orthoclase	36.17
Soda ash	4.38
Manganese dioxide	2.28
Red iron oixde	2.31
	99.97

Note: It may be observed that the orthoclase (the only available feldspar that would most nearly fit the K$_2$O, Al$_2$O$_3$, and SiO$_2$ requirements of the empirical formula) imports into the recipe a bit too much SiO$_2$, an excess of .1638 molecular equivalents, in fact. However, in a glaze like KCC#3, for example, using 10% of pine ash, the discrepancy or excess of silica would be only 0.666% for each 100 units of batch weight, a rather negligible amount. Only when much greater proportions of pine ash than 10% are needed would it be necessary to subtract some flint from the batch.

Results from Use of Synthetic Wood Ash in Glazes

To date, my experiments with the incorporation of my two synthetic wood ash substitutes into several of my regular stoneware glazes have been rather encouraging. In the case of a Chün glaze like CIH-p, for example, my synthetic "pine ash" produced a range of colors and textures, from a handsome, bright blue translucent to a blue-gray stony matte, successful enough to justify some comparison with my usual results with natural pine ash. In addition, the color of a "synthetic" KCC#3 glaze represented a bona fide celadon, more or less approximating that of the real thing, though not quite so blue in tinge nor so unctuous in texture as the Koryo-like quality of the original KCC#3. As for my synthetic "mixed-wood" ash, when used in place of my regular natural ash in CIH-m, it yielded yet another blue-tinged stony matte, even if somewhat drier in texture.

Thus, it is now clear to me that anyone deprived of the natural sources of supply for "wood ash" material might still be able to ring a great number of attractive changes on the themes of celadon, Chün, and much else besides. It will certainly be worthwhile to add these "synthetics" to one's arsenal of ceramic possibilities, along with their *natural* progenitors.

For myself, of course, my preference will always be for the latter. Not only are they the superior originals for use in superior quality glazes, but they are still comparatively simpler to prepare and work with.

APPENDIX

Ball Mill Construction

Since I have frequently indicated the use of a ball mill as being essential to the preparation of many of the glazes explained in this book, a brief account of how to make and use one may be useful.

Components Needed

1. An electric motor, 1/4 or 1/3 h.p., 1725–1750 r.p.m.

2. One 1½″ motor pulley.

3. One 3½″ motor pulley.

4. One short pulley belt (about 25″).

5. One ¾″ thick wooden board, 28″ long by 16″ wide.

6. Two wooden 3x3s about 15½″ long. (If 3x3s are unavailable, 2x4s may be substituted.)

7. Four pillow blocks with ½″ shaft openings.

8. Two ½″ steel shaft rods, one about 18″ long, the other about 17″ long. (If you can, substitute for the 17″ rod an old rubber washing-machine roller about 13½″ to 14″ long with ½″ wide steel rod tips extending beyond each end.)

9. Two 12″ lengths of ½″ plastic (or rubber) tubing to cover the middle 12″ portion of each steel shaft rod. (Only one length is needed if you are substituting a washing-machine roller for one of the rods.)

10. Three ½″ rod collars. (Only one is needed if a washing-machine roller is being used.)

11. Eight 2″ wood screws; eight 1¼″ wood screws; four 1¼″ bolts (or ¾″ wood screws, if preferred).

12. One gallon (or, preferably, 5 quart) cylindrical, stoneware, ball mill jar containing about 3 pounds of flint pebbles. You can either purchase one or throw one on the wheel yourself, using a dense, fine-textured stoneware clay, and fire it unglazed to cone 10 (see accompanying drawing). A stoneware lid can easily be designed to make a tight fit over the wide recessed jar mouth; it can be clamped firmly in place by means of a strong metal bail attached to the collar of the jar on two sides. The underside of the lid should be cushioned against the mouth of the jar by means of a foam rubber pad cut in a circle slightly larger than the mouth opening. This pad, in turn, can be shielded from the different glaze batches by being wrapped in disposable sheets of thin plastic.

Directions for Assembling the Components

1. Secure the two 3x3s across the wooden board at one of its ends, leaving a space of 4″ between them. (If using two 2x4s, leave a space of 3¼″ between them.) Use the 2″ wood screws, countersunk from the *under*side of the wooden board, to fasten the two pieces in place, four screws to a piece.

2. Mount the four pillow blocks on the two 3x3s, two on each 3x3 at its opposite ends. Align each pillow block so that the center lubricating hole atop each is exactly 7″ away from that of the pillow block nearest it on the nearby 3x3. Thus the four pillow blocks will be exactly parallel to each other and will form an exact rectangle. (This is most important, since the steel shaft rods must be able to slip easily through the ½″ center holes of *both* pillow blocks mounted on each 3x3.) Use the eight

Plan of Ball Mill

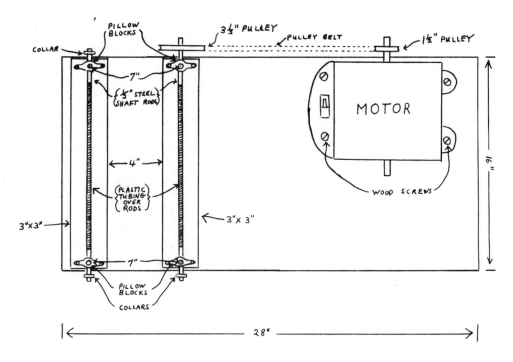

Design for Ball Mill Jar

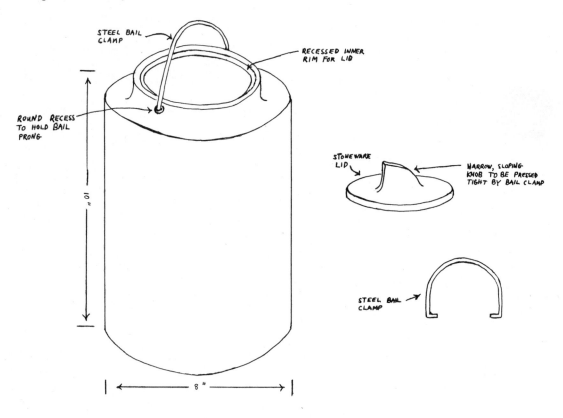

1¼″ wood screws to secure the pillow blocks in place. However, wait until the next step is completed before *permanently* securing *one* pillow block of each pair.

3. Slide the plastic tubing onto each steel shaft rod, and center the tubing. This will be easier to do if you first lubricate the rod or the inside of the tubing with soapy water.

4. Insert one bare end of the shorter (17″) steel shaft rod into the center ½″ hole of the one already secured pillow block on the *endmost* 3x3. Then run the unsecured pillow block onto the opposite bare end of the same rod, and screw this pillow block into its already marked place. Be sure that each end of the rod projects enough on the outer side of each pillow block to permit a collar to be fastened to it. (If you are using a washing-machine roller, instead, no projection of the steel center is needed, and therefore no collars are needed here, either.)

5. Similarly, insert the longer (18″) steel shaft rod into the center ½″ hole of the pillow block secured on the second 3x3, and run the unsecured pillow block onto the rod's opposite end. Screw this pillow block into its marked place.

6. Tightly fasten the 3½″ pulley onto the longer protruding end of the second (18″) steel shaft rod. (A set screw is usually provided with a pulley for this purpose.)

7. Secure a ½″ collar to each of the other protruding steel shaft rod ends.

8. Securely fasten the 1½″ motor pulley to the electric motor shaft.

9. Place the electric motor on the wooden board with the two pulleys lined up with each other.

10. Run the pulley belt around both the 3½″ pulley and the 1½″ pulley so that it is quite taut. This arrangement will result in the electric motor's being at a slight distance from the nearer 3x3 and well over toward one edge of the wooden board.

11. Securely fasten the electric motor in place at the point required by step 10. Use either ¾″ wood screws or, preferably, 1¼″ bolts countersunk from the underside of the board.

Another very satisfactory arrangement is to mount the electric motor on its own separate board. Thus, each time the ball mill is to be used, the motor can be repositioned by means of the pulley belt, and then clamped in place with a large C clamp that also serves to hold the entire unit to a work table.

12. Lubricate the four pillow blocks with a few drops of motor oil.

Using the Ball Mill

1. Lay the locked-up ball mill jar with its charge of glaze ingredients, pebbles, and water in the cradle formed by the two padded steel shaft rods. (If you are dry-milling, omit the water, of course.) In any case, do not overfill the jar. For a 5 quart jar, a glaze ingredient charge of no more than 2000 grams would be about right. This, together with the pebbles and water, would still leave enough head room to ensure efficient grinding.

2. Plug the electric motor cord into an electrical outlet, and flip the motor switch.

3. Rotative power is transmitted from the motor pulley to the first steel rod which, through the constant physical contact among the movable parts, causes the ball jar and, in turn, the second rod (or roller) to revolve. Thus, the two rods spin in the same direction as each other, and the jar cradled between them rotates in the opposite direction.

4. After a dozen or so revolutions of the jar, stop the motor, lift the mill upright out of its cradle, remove the jar lid, and inspect the state of the charge.

5. If the charge is too dry, add a very small amount of water, and repeat the three previous steps. For best grinding results, the glaze mix should have the appearance of thick cream. If the mix is too dry, no grinding will occur. If the mix is too watery, the grinding will be inefficient and will also cause excessive wear of the inside of the ball mill jar.

6. Mill for no more than the time indicated in the text for each glaze.

GLOSSARY

Acids. The principal acid components of ceramic glazes are silica (SiO_2) and boric oxide (B_2O_3). The feldspathic glazes of Sung times are rich in silica and therefore require higher temperatures for maturing than do predominantly alkaline glazes. Color is also strongly influenced by the relatively heavy proportion of acid over alkaline components in a glaze, or vice versa.

Alkalies. A term that in the most restrictive sense refers to compounds of sodium, potassium, and lithium. In ceramics, it also serves to include the alkaline earths, which are compounds containing calcium, magnesium, barium, zinc, and lead. All are important fluxes in various eutectic combinations. Glazes in which the proportion of alkalies is relatively high mature at lower temperatures. They also have a greater tendency to craze.

Alumina (Al_2O_3). A very refractory, white substance naturally occurring as a constituent of clay and feldspar, as well as other minerals. (See *Kaolin*.)

Ball Clay. A fine-textured, very plastic clay of moderate to high refractoriness which fires to either a white or cream color. In small proportions, it is useful as a component of clay bodies and slips. A typical percentage analysis of it is: SiO_2 51.92, Al_2O_3 31.78, Fe_2O_3 .87, TiO_2 1.52, CaO .21, MgO .19, Na_2O .38, K_2O .89, L.O.I. 12.29.

Ball Mill. A rotating device for grinding the components of a glaze mixture to finer grain size. The grinding media used are either flint pebbles or porcelain cylinders. (See the plans for how to construct and use a ball mill.)

Batch Recipe. The formula for a glaze in terms of ceramic raw materials (kaolin, whiting, feldspar, flint, etc.) to be weighed out and mixed together.

Bisque. Ware that has been low fired once without glaze to increase its permeability and facilitate handling and glazing before the final glaze firing, usually at higher temperatures.

Body. The clay, or mixture of clays and other substances like feldspar and flint, from which pottery is made.

Boron. An element of important use in several kinds of glazes. It not only adds to the fusibility of a glaze and the brilliancy of its surface, but it is strongly solvent of colorant oxides. Thus, it is especially useful in such glazes as oxblood and peach bloom. (See *Colemanite*.)

Calcium Carbonate ($CaCO_3$). A base of great importance as a fluxing agent in glazes, especially medium and high temperature compositions. It is added to ceramic bodies and glazes most directly in the form of whiting. When used in excess of certain proportions in a glaze, it contributes to the formation of a microcrystalline matte texture. (See *Whiting*.)

Celadon. Term applied to a wide variety of stonewares, the glazes of which range in hue from gray and green to blue-green, blue, and olive green. The oxide responsible for these colors is iron in various degrees of concentration and reduction. The name is apparently French in origin, having been given to the ware at the time when a particular shade of green was in vogue in 17th century France because of the gray-green costumes worn by the character Celadon, who was Astrée's lover in d'Urfé's *L'Astrée*.

Ch'ing. Name applied to the Manchu dynasty (1644–1912). Among many other wares characteristic of this period, it is famous for the ox-blood (sang-de-boeuf) and peach bloom glazes produced during the reign of K'ang Hsi in the early part of the 18th century.

Ch'ing-pai. See *Ying Ch'ing*.

Chün. Actually, a special variety of Sung celadon with a distinctively opalescent, bluish cast. (There are also instances of green Chün, as well as of lavender-gray.) The opalescent color is apparently owing to the formation of ferrous phosphate in the fired glaze. Many Chün specimens also bear splashes of reduced copper red; others have a suffusion of copper red over most of their surfaces, and often verge on purple. The essential, basic color, though, is a reduced iron blue.

Clay. A plastic substance of which the essential constituents are hydrated silicates of aluminum. It is formed by the decomposition and alteration of feldspathic rocks. There are many types of clay, classified according to relative plasticity, refractoriness, density, non-plastic components, color, fluxing impurities contained, and vitrification capabilities. Not only is clay the predominant component of all ceramic ware bodies, but in one form or other, it is almost indispensable as a glaze constituent. One noteworthy exception to this general rule is turquoise glaze. (See *Kaolin*.)

Cobalt Oxide (CoO). A colorant of very high tinctorial power, producing varying shades of somewhat harsh blue in glazes of different composition and at all temperatures. A relatively impure cobalt ore used in underglaze painting in the blue-and-white ware of the Ming period created a warmer, less staring effect.

Colemanite (2CaO, 3B$_2$O$_3$, 5H$_2$O). A natural hydrated calcium borate, only slightly soluble in water. It is useful as a means of introducing boron into a glaze instead of resorting to completely soluble boron compounds like borax or boric acid. A glaze of which it is a component is best mixed dry, so as to avoid excessive crystallization of the unused batch induced by the colemanite during long periods of standing in a container. (See *Boron*.)

Cones. (References throughout this book are to Orton standard pyrometric cones.) Devices for measuring the work-heat in kilns during firing. Shaped in the form of tall, three-sided pyramids, slightly tilted to one side, they are made of glaze components calcuated to bend or deform at various anticipated temperatures or work-heats and in accordance with the rate of heat rise per hour. Each such composition bears an identifying number; for example, when fired at about 300°F. (167°C.) per hour, cone 06 corresponds to approximately 1859°F. (1015°C.), a bisquing or low-fire glaze heat, whereas cone 8 corresponds to about 2300°F., (1260°C.) a point at which stoneware glazes and bodies mature.

Copper Oxide (CuO). Next to iron, the most important colorant in ceramics. Depending on proportion, glaze composition, and firing technique, it can yield a wide variety of greens, blues, turquoises, blue-greens, pinks, and reds.

Cornwall (Cornish) Stone. A granite rock of varying chemical composition whose main constituents are feldspar and quartz, together with a wide assortment of other minerals like fluorspar, mica, kaolin, lime, alkalies, magnesia, etc. In England, it is much used both in bodies and in glazes, functioning in much the same way as a feldspar, though larger proportions are generally needed. It is also valuable in the preparation of slips, improving their adhesiveness.

Crackle. Minute cracks or craze marks in a fired glaze that form irregular lines in various net-like patterns. These are frequently emphasized after firing either by deliberate staining for decorative effect or by daily use of the ware, or, if the glaze contains ferrous phosphate, by the effect of aerial oxygen. (See *Crazing*.)

Crazing. Cracking of a glaze after firing, either at once or over varying periods of time. It is caused by significant differences in the rate of expansion and contraction of a glaze and that of the body on which it has been fired. (See section on *Crackle* in Chapter 3.)

Devitrification. The loss of "glassiness" (vitrification) in a glaze. Strictly speaking, it refers to changes in the structure of a glaze whereby small crystals form in it. The resulting appearance of the glaze may be either increased opacity or a microcrystalline matte texture. The term is also loosely applied to describe the appearance of dull-surfaced glazes in which there are significant amounts of undissolved oxides.

Dunting. The cracking and subsequent breakage of a piece of pottery, either while the kiln is cooling, or when it has shortly been removed from the kiln, or when it has been out of the kiln for hours and even days. Cold air draughts on the hot ware are sometimes responsible, but a more fundamental cause is the rupturing of the ware body by the constrictive force of a fired glaze that encases it. In the latter case, the composition of either the body or the glaze must be changed in later trials. An especially interesting observation I have noted about dunting is that it almost always takes the form of a *spiral* that goes *upward*, particularly on bottles and vases, in the *same direction* as the pull of the potter's fingers when he originally threw the piece on the wheel.

Empirical Formula. The molecular formula of the chemical components in a glaze. It is used as the basis for establishing a corresponding formula, or batch recipe, in terms of ceramic raw materials or compounds. The empirical formula is arranged in three groups: the RO monoxide group, consisting of alkalies and bases computed to a total of 1.0000 (or unity); the R$_2$O$_3$ sesquioxide group, consisting of compounds like alumina (Al$_2$O$_3$) that can serve as both acids and bases; and the RO$_2$ dioxide group, normally containing the acid, silica (SiO$_2$).

Epidote. A common mineral composed of calcium, iron, alumina, and silica. In color it varies from pistachio green to blackish green and light yellow brown. It is found in a wide variety of metamorphic rocks, altered igneous rocks, pegmatites, and trap rock.

Eutectic. A combination of substances that fuses at a lower temperature than any other combination of the same constituents. This temperature, called the *eutectic point*, is lower than the melting point of any one of the separate constituents.

Feldspar. An essential mineral component of all stoneware and porcelain bodies, and equally indispensable to Sung-type glazes. In nature, the various feldspars are the principal constituents of igneous and plutonic rocks, and their crystals can be seen most commonly in the different granites. There are three groups of feldspar: orthoclase, microcline, and plagioclase. Of these, the first two are potassium aluminum silicates; the third includes a range of sub-types containing different mixtures of sodium and calcium aluminum silicates.

Feldspathic Glaze. A stoneware or porcelain glaze containing a relatively high proportion of feldspar. Glazes of this type, unlike lead or high alkaline glazes, are very resistant to disintegration, even when buried in the ground for centuries. (See *Feldspar*.)

Fire Clay. A relatively refractory clay, owing to the greater percentage of alumina it contains in proportion to fluxes and to *free* silica (as differentiated from the silica in the compound, aluminum silicate).

Flint. A microcrystalline form of silica (SiO_2) which is prepared for ceramic use by calcining and grinding. Sources may vary from flint pebbles to quartz, quartzite, sand, or sandstone. Flint is generally used as a raw material to add free silica to ware bodies and to glaze compositions. (See *Silica*.)

Flux. A substance that tends to lower the point of fusibility of any ceramic mixture of which it is a part. Chief among the fluxes are sodium, potassium, calcium, lithium, magnesium, barium, zinc, and lead.

Granite. The commonest coarse-grained rock of igneous origin, it is composed of quartz (free silica), feldspar, and isolated grains of a dark mineral such as mica or pyroxene. The nature of the feldspar content may be any one of the three groups: orthoclase, microcline, or plagioclase. Some granites may function like feldspars in bodies and in glazes. (See *Feldspar* and *Cornwall Stone*.)

Greenware. Pottery that has been thrown and turned, or otherwise formed, dried, but not yet fired.

Hare's Fur. A variety of temmoku in which the glaze forms streaks of opaque light brown, sometimes with a hint of gray or blue-gray, against a background of dark blackish brown of glassier consistency. The pattern made by the streaks as the viscous glaze flows toward the foot of a piece bears a resemblance to hare's fur, or, in some views, partridge feathers.

Interface. The zone of contact between a glaze and the body on which it has been fired. Microsections of fired stoneware reveal that crystals often grow into the glaze from the body or vice versa. The degree of interaction between the two depends on a large number of variables, such as glaze and body composition (and the relative solubility of their components), thickness of glaze application, porosity of the bisque, firing conditions, and viscosity of the melting glaze. Ideally, the interface in fired stoneware should be a vaguely defined area in cross-section, rather than a sharp demarcation between body and glaze. One of the drawbacks of the latter condition is a strong tendency on the part of the glaze to craze or shiver. Conversely, an interfacial zone created by the mutual interaction and deep interpenetration of glaze and body promotes stability in the ware.

Iron Oxide (Fe_2O_3). Probably the most valuable ceramic colorant of all. Depending on its use in different proportions, glaze compositions, and patterns of firing, it can help produce yellows, tans, browns, reds, blacks, grays, greens, blue-greens, and blues. It also acts as a catalyst, though not so powerfully as tin oxide, to the formation of colloidal copper in reduced copper red glazes.

Jordan Clay. A stoneware clay that fires buff in oxidation, gray or brown in reduction. It is frequently the principal component of stoneware bodies. A representative percentage analysis of it is: SiO_2 67.19, Al_2O_3 20.23, Fe_2O_3 1.73, TiO_2 1.18, CaO .16, MgO .52, Na_2O .23, K_2O 2.0, L.O.I. 6.89.

Ju. (Pronounced *roo*.) Almost legendary Sung celadon ware of which only a few authenticated specimens survive. It was made either at Juchou or within the palace enclosure at K'ai-fêng for only a few years early in the 12th century. It has been described and pictured variously, most often as a smooth, opaque bluish green, sometimes with a suggestion of lavender.

K'ang Hsi. A Ch'ing dynasty emperor in the early part of the 18th century. His name has been applied to a number of wares produced during his reign at Ching-tê Chên, a large ceramic metropolis in Kiangsi province. These wares include blue-and-white porcelains, enameled porcelains, and the famous copper red porcelains, sang-de-boeuf (oxblood) and peach bloom.

Kaolin or China Clay (Al_2O_3, $2SiO_2$, $2H_2O$). A major component, together with feldspar, of Oriental porcelain bodies. It is also the generally preferred type of clay for use in glazes. Of relatively great purity, it is the most refractory of all clays. The almost pure alumina it brings to a glaze mixture significantly helps to control and stabilize its fusibility and fluidity. The higher the proportion of kaolin in a glaze, the less the fusibility, a factor that is useful in producing microcrystalline matte surfaces. Its use is to be avoided in turquoise glazes, however, as it destroys the color. A representative percentage analysis of Georgia kaolin is: SiO_2 45.20, Al_2O_3 38.02, Fe_2O_3 .49, TiO_2 1.95, CaO .26, MgO .30, Na_2O .02, K_2O .04, L.O.I. 13.51.

K-brick. High Temperature Insulating brick.

Kinuta. Japanese name for blue-green celadon of Lung-ch'üan type. (See *Lung-ch'üan*.)

Ko. A Sung celadon with stained crackle. (See *Kuan*.)

Koryo. A Korean dynasty (936–1392 A.D.), roughly contemporaneous with the Chinese Sung and Yüan, during which especially fine celadons were produced, particularly in the first half of the 12th century. The typical Koryo celadon glaze is a rich, semi-transparent, blue-green somewhat darker in hue than Kuan or Lung-ch'üan.

Kuan. Literally, "imperial ware" (i.e. for imperial or palace use during the Sung era). Its glaze varies from a polished stone effect to a gem-like quality, the color likewise going from a whitish gray or a gray-green to a translucent blue. Different specimens may be either uncrazed or crackled. The latter, when stained, were formerly referred to as "Ko" ware.

Lime (CaO). Strictly speaking, a white caustic earth (calcium oxide) got by burning limestone. The term is applied rather freely to many different substances supplying the important base, calcium carbonate, to a glaze. (See *Calcium Carbonate* and *Whiting*.)

Lithium Carbonate (Li_2CO_3). A chemically prepared source of the metal, lithium, providing a much richer concentration of it than is available in natural lithium ores (like amblygonite, spodumene, lepidolite) which contain less than 10% of the metal. Spectroscopic analysis has indicated its presence in Ying-Ch'ing ("shadow-blue") ware of Sung times. It was apparently present, also, in other blue celadons as a trace mineral that helped intensify the color.

Local Reduction. A method (developed by Arthur E. Baggs and Edgar Littlefield at Ohio State University) of achieving reduction of colorant oxides like copper or iron in a glaze, during normally oxidizing fire. The means used is the addition of a small proportion of such materials as silicon carbide into the glaze mixture. Such materials are sufficiently refractory to remain stable until, at stoneware temperatures, they release carbon into the glaze and thus simulate reducing conditions for a limited period of the firing cycle. The glazes involved must not be viscous, or the fired results will be seriously cratered. The method is most often used as one means of achieving copper red effects. (See *Silicon Carbide*.)

L.O.I. Abbreviation for loss on ignition, or the percentage of loss in weight of a sample of material heated under specific conditions. In glaze calculation, it refers to the percentage of water and carbonaceous material in a component substance. It is therefore calculated as water (H_2O). The function of the molecular equivalent of H_2O is limited solely to helping calculate the total molecular weight of a substance (see Chapter 12). Beyond that, it is not needed in calculating glaze formulas.

Lung-ch'üan. A very productive pottery center in Chekiang province, the name of which became assimilated to a variety of pale bluish green celadon made there and quite widely marketed. A special type of it became known by

Japanese connoisseurs as "Kinuta" (mallet) after a much admired mallet-shaped celadon vase of Lung-ch'üan provenance.

Magnesium Carbonate ($MgCO_3$). In lower temperatures, a relatively refractory base, as compared with calcium carbonate. With higher temperature glazes, however, it becomes a strong fluxing agent. At certain ranges in particular glaze mixtures, it tends to produce opacity, as well as to promote glossiness.

Manganese Dioxide. An oxide used in bodies to promote a brown, black, or purplish color. In various glazes, it produces browns, violet-purples, and, in combination with cobalt and iron, blacks. It is also a very useful component of black underglazes.

Ming. A Chinese dynasty (1368--1643 A.D.) during which increasingly sophisticated control over potting, glazing, and decorating techniques began to manifest itself at some expense to the more "natural" qualities inherent in Sung ceramics. Great strides were made in the production of porcelain bodies and glazes. Perhaps the most distinguished wares were the blue-and-white and the Hsüan-tê copper reds.

Muffle. A highly refractory wall, chamber, or container inside a kiln which separates the ware from direct contact with the flames. A half-muffle represents the lower half or less of such a chamber and is open on top.

Nepheline Syenite. A pale-colored rock similar to granite, except that it contains no quartz. However, it is rich both in feldspar and syenite, a feldspathoid mineral. A representative percentage analysis of nepheline syenite is: SiO_2 60.22, Al_2O_3 23.72, Fe_2O_3 .06, CaO .42, MgO .09, Na_2O 10.06, K_2O 5.04, L.O.I. .47.

Northern Celadon. Term applied to a rather glassy, thinly glazed, olive green Sung celadon of no precisely known provenance. It is usually decorated with carved or impressed floral patterns under the glaze. The glaze color has been variously attributed to partial reduction of the glaze (combining Fe_2O_3 with FeO) and to the large amount of iron used as colorant in a highly acid glaze. It has also been conjectured that the principal fuel used in firing was coal (available in northern China); hence the tendency to oxidize and only partly reduce the glaze. In my view, the acidity is the more likely explanation, since the color generally runs to browner greens with extra increments of iron.

Oil Spot. A variety of temmoku in which the surface of the brown-black glaze is dotted with silvery spots of various sizes. The spots are probably formed by bubbles that have burst on the surface of the glaze during firing, leaving pits into which then flow the more soluble and iron-rich elements of the contiguous portions of the glaze. When cooled, these spots are actually crystallized formations in the glaze.

Oxblood or Sang-de-Boeuf. A deep red glaze, obtained from reduced copper as the glaze colorant, which requires a sufficiency of aerial oxygen at certain stages of the firing to bring out the best color.

Oxidation. The method of firing a kiln with enough oxygen present in the kiln atmosphere to ensure the complete combustion of the fuel gases. Accordingly, the metals present in both the clay and the glaze remain or become oxides, giving the fired result the characteristic coloring of these in combination with the other oxides variously present in the composition.

Peach Bloom. A reduced copper glaze with a soft pink matrix in which there float spots and passages of deep red and, in some cases, occasional spots of green.

Phosphorus. Chemical analysis has shown that this element, in the form of phosphoric acid (P_2O_5), is present in a great number of Sung glazes, probably owing to the use of wood ash in the glaze mixture. It not only tends to lend some opacity to a glaze, mainly because of the gas bubbles it creates during firing, but it also contributes significantly in combination with reduced iron (forming ferrous phosphate) to the blue tints of celadons and Chün.

Potassium Oxide. One of the two principal alkalies in ceramic use. (See *Sodium Oxide*.) A very important fluxing agent, it is much less active than sodium, decreases glaze fluidity and crazing, and increases its durability. Excessive proportions of it, however, may cause peeling or crazing of the glaze. It is most easily available for glaze batches as a constituent of feldspars.

Redart Clay. An iron-rich earthenware clay produced by the Cedar Heights Clay Company of Ohio that can be successfully incorporated in stoneware body compositions. Its percentage analysis is reported to be: SiO_2 64.27, Al_2O_3 16.41, Fe_2O_3 7.04, TiO_2 1.06, CaO .23, MgO 1.55, Na_2O .40, K_2O 4.07, L.O.I. 4.78.

Reduction. The process of firing a kiln so as to exclude much of the oxygen normally added to its atmosphere by air. Thus, combustion is incomplete and smoky, and the carbon monoxide and hydrocarbon gases present in the kiln atmosphere "steal" oxygen from the oxides in both the body and the glaze of the ware being fired. These oxides are thereby "reduced" to lower oxides (e.g. Fe_2O_3 may become Fe_3O_4 or FeO) or even to the metal itself (e.g. Fe), causing changes in their color and textural characteristics.

Refractory. Descriptive of a substance that is resistant to softening or melting at high temperatures.

Resists. Materials such as wax, paraffin, or paper that are decoratively applied to parts of the surface of ware to prevent the adherence of particular layers of slip, coloring oxide, or glaze. Designs and contrasts in color and texture are thus achieved.

Sang-de-Boeuf. (See *Oxblood*.)

Silica (SiO_2). The most abundant and predominant substance in all aspects of ceramics, constituting more than 50% of the content of most glazes. The chief acidic component in glazes, it combines readily with a wide variety of other oxides, particularly the alkalies and other bases, thereby creating a great number of different silicates. Depending on eutectic factors, increased silica content in a glaze generally will make it more refractory, decrease its fluidity, lessen its tendency to craze, and increase its hardness. (See *Flint*.)

Silicon Carbide (SiC). A synthetically prepared material that has proved useful in the production of copper red glazes when fired in an oxidizing atmosphere. (See *Local Reduction*.)

Slip or Engobe. A liquid clay or clays, sometimes with the addition of fluxes and non-plastics like feldspar, whiting, flint). Besides its use in mold casting, it is most frequently employed as a thin coating over all or part of a ceramic body, either to provide a different colored surface under a glaze, to cover up surface defects in the body, to provide a suitable background for underglaze brushwork decoration, or to serve as a layer through which designs may be cut to the body.

Slip Glaze. A glaze usually containing a large proportion of clay or clay-like crushed rocks (slate, shale) that tend to flux at temperatures usually required for glaze maturation. In some cases, the slip glaze consists solely of a natural clay whose high content of fluxing impurities enables it to fire at relatively low temperatures and produce a brownish or greenish glaze. One familiar example of this type is Albany Slip, a natural clay dug in the vicinity of Albany, N.Y.

Soak. The maintaining of work-heat at a specific level for a limited portion of the firing schedule to achieve a particular glaze effect.

Sodium Oxide (Na_2O). One of the two principal alkalies in ceramic use. (See *Potassium Oxide*.) It is especially valuable as a fluxing agent for silica and borax. However, large proportions of it tend to increase crazing and excessive glaze fluidity, as well as to lessen its durability. It is present in various feldspars and is the main component of soda ash (Na_2CO_3).

Stoneware. Ware composed of clay, feldspar, and quartz that has been fired to the point of complete or partial vitrification, usually at temperatures ranging between 2240°F. (1227°C.) and 2400°F. (1316°C.).

Sung. The Chinese dynasty (960–1279 A.D.) during which a wide variety of largely monochrome stonewares and porcelains was developed to great heights of aesthetic achievement. Outstanding among its wares are the best examples of Kuan, Ko, Lung-ch'üan, Chün, Ju, Northern Celadon, Ying Ch'ing, temmoku, Ting, and Tz'u-chou.

Temmoku. Japanese name for Chien yao, a brown or black iron-rich slip-glazed ware produced in Sung times in Fukien province, as well as in Honan and Kiangsi. The various effects include plain brown or black, "oil spot," and "hare's fur." (See *Oil Spot, Hare's Fur*.)

Tin Oxide (SnO$_2$). Normally used as a strong opacifier in glazes, it is especially interesting for its role in promoting, much more powerfully than iron oxide, the formation of colloidal copper in reduced copper red glazes.

Ting. A white porcelain ware made in Sung times, and named after the town where it was produced. There are also rare examples of black- or brown-glazed Ting.

Trap Rock. The commercial name for crushed basalt, a fine-grained rock consisting mainly of plagioclase (calcium-sodium feldspar), pyroxenes, and olivine. It contains no quartz.

Turquoise. An alkaline oxidized copper glaze of a brilliant light blue with just a suggestion of green. The color is best achieved in the relative absence of alumina; calcium and magnesium should also be avoided. (See *Kaolin*.)

Tz'u-chou. Literally, "Pottery Town," the name of a pottery center in Hopei province with a very long history of ceramic production. The ware typically associated with the name is brush decorated in black on a white slip ground with a covering of thin, transparent glaze. Other varieties include carved decoration through either brown or white slip, as well as monochromatic brown and black glazed ware.

Viscosity. The characteristic of a glaze in the process of being fired that promotes its adherence to the ware and stabilizes its thickness to relative uniformity. An insufficiently viscous glaze will drain off inclined surfaces and will puddle at the base of the ware. A glaze of high viscosity, even when applied thickly and fired at high temperatures, will have very little vertical flow. An intermediate example of a glaze with high viscosity but a certain amount of controlled flow is the typical hare's fur temmoku with its characteristic thick roll of glaze collecting slightly above the foot of the ware.

Volcanic Ash. In glaze formulations, this material can serve in somewhat the same way as granite powder. A rule of thumb for its use is that it can roughly substitute for 70% of the feldspar and 30% of the flint needed in a batch recipe. A typical empirical formula of volcanic ash is: .660 K$_2$O, .230 Na$_2$O, .096 CaO, .014

MgO, .899 Al$_2$O$_3$, .060 Fe$_2$O$_3$, 9.59 SiO$_2$, and .05 TiO$_2$.

Whiting. For ceramic purposes, this form of calcium carbonate is a finely ground white powder from any one of several sources, including English cliffstone (chalk), limestone, and chemically precipitated calcium carbonate. (See *Calcium Carbonate*.)

Wood Ash. An important fluxing agent in Far Eastern stoneware glazes. Of variable chemical composition, it is normally rich in silica and calcium carbonate, is a valuable source of phosphorus, and contains significant proportions of magnesium, potassium, and sodium, as well as some alumina and traces of iron and other oxides. Careful washing of the ash eliminates unwanted substances like soluble potash, sulphates, and chlorides.

Work-heat. The actual heat at work in the maturation of a glaze or body, as contrasted with the numerical indications of kiln temperature given by a thermocoupled pyrometer. The effective work-heat in separate firings to the same indicated temperatures can therefore differ considerably because of such variants as the rate and uniformity of heating, the stacking pattern and volume, and the total length of time involved in each firing. To some extent, especially because of this last factor, work-heat can even differ from the indications signalized by pyrometric cones. (See *Cones*.)

Worm Tracks. A fanciful name for the small, irregular markings in the surface of a matured Chün or celadon glaze that survive from the fissures and cracks that normally open up in it during the earlier stages of firing. As the firing continues, the more fluid elements in the glaze flow into these fissures and "heal" them. The sites of the former cracks are thus faintly revealed by the resultant color differences between them and the surrounding glaze areas.

Yellow Ochre. A hydrated iron-bearing natural earth very useful as a colorant in celadon and Chün glazes, as a pigment for brushwork on or under glazes, or as a stain for bodies and slips.

Ying Ch'ing. (The term means "shadow blue.") A Sung dynasty porcelain ware characterized by a glaze that is faintly blue where it runs thick. More recently, the name, Ch'ing-pai has also been applied to this ware.

Zinc Oxide (ZnO). An important flux in certain kinds of glazes. It is an indispensable component of the so-called Bristol glaze, a soft stoneware temperature porcelain type, to which it lends, together with alumina, both opacity and whiteness. Zinc oxide is also credited with the prevention of crazing and the increased brilliance of certain colors, except for strong blues or greens.

BIBLIOGRAPHY

A. I. Andrews, *Ceramic Tests and Calculations*. New York: J. Wiley and Sons, 1928.

J. N. Collie, "Notes on Some Chinese Glazes on Pottery and Porcelain," *Transactions of the British Ceramic Society*, vol. 15, 1915-1916, pp. 160-165.

——————, "Notes on the Sang-de-Boeuf and the Copper-Red Chinese Glazes," *Transactions of the British Ceramic Society*, vol. 17, 1917-1918, pp. 379-384.

Paul E. Cox, "A Very White Glaze for Stoneware," *Ceramic Age*, Newark, vol. 66, no. 3, September 1955, pp. 41-42.

Warren E. Cox, *The Book of Pottery and Porcelain*. 2 vols., New York: Crown, 1944.

Père D'Entrecolles, "Letters of Père D'Entrecolles," (1712 and 1722), translated in William Burton, *Porcelain, A Sketch of Its Nature, Art, and Manufacture*. London: Cassell and Co., 1906, pp. 84-122.

Sir Harry Garner, "Ju and Kuan Wares of the Sung Dynasty," *The Burlington Magazine*, London, vol. 94, no. 597, December 1952, pp. 349-352.

G. St. G. M. Gompertz, *Chinese Celadon Wares*. London: Faber and Faber, 1958.

——————, *Korean Celadon and Other Wares of the Koryo Period*. London: Faber and Faber, 1963.

——————, *Korean Pottery and Porcelain of the Yi Period*. New York: Praeger, 1968.

Basil Gray, *Early Chinese Pottery and Porcelain*. London: Faber and Faber, 1953.

C. M. Harder, "Red Glazes and Underglaze Red by Reduction," *Journal of the American Ceramic Society*, vol. 19, no. 1, January 1936, pp. 26-28.

Seizo Hayashiga and Gakuji Hasebe, *Chinese Ceramics*. Rutland, Vt.: Charles Tuttle Co., 1966.

Arthur L. Hetherington, *Chinese Ceramic Glazes*. 2nd rev. ed., Los Angeles: The Commonwealth Press, 1948.

——————, *The Early Ceramic Wares of China*. London: Benn Bros., 1922.

Robert L. Hobson and Arthur L. Hetherington, *The Art of the Chinese Potter*. New York: Alfred Knopf, 1923.

Robert L. Hobson, *Chinese Pottery and Porcelain in the Percival David Collection*. London: The Stourton Press, 1934.

William B. Honey, *The Art of the Potter*. London: Faber and Faber, 1946.

——————, *Corean Pottery*. New York: D. Van Nostrand Co., 1948.

Tsuneshi Ishii, "Experiments on the Kinuta Blue Celadon Glaze," *Transactions of the British Ceramic Society*, vol. 29, May 1930, pp. 360-387.

Fujio Koyama and John Figgess, *Two Thousand Years of Oriental Ceramics*. New York: Abrams, 1961.

Berthold Laufer, *The Beginnings of Porcelain in China (With a Technical Report by H. W. Nichols)*. Chicago: Field Museum of Natural History, Publication 192, vol. 15, no. 2, 1917, pp. 79-183.

Bernard Leach, *A Potter's Book*. London: Faber and Faber, 1946. Levittown, N.Y.: Transatlantic, 1973.

Edgar Littlefield, "Local Reduction Copper Reds," *Ceramic Monthly*, Columbus, Ohio, vol. 1, no. 12, December 1953, pp. 16-18.

Joseph W. Mellor, "The Chemistry of the Chinese Copper-Red Glazes, Parts I and II," *Transactions of the British Ceramic Society*, vol. 35, 1936, pp. 364-378; 487-491.

R. T. Paine and W. J. Young, "A Preliminary Report on the Sub-Surface Structure of Glazes of Kuan and Kuan-type Wares," *Far Eastern Ceramic Bulletin*, Cambridge, Mass., vol. 5, no. 3, September, 1953.

Cullen W. Parmelee, *Ceramic Glazes*. 2nd rev. ed., Chicago: Industrial Publications, 1951.

Daniel Rhodes, *Clay and Glazes for the Potter*. New York: Greenberg, 1957. London: Pitman, 1967.

——————, *Stoneware and Porcelain, the Art of High-Fired Pottery*. Philadelphia: Chilton, 1959. London: Pitman, 1960.

Herbert H. Sanders, *The World of Japanese Ceramics*. Tokyo and Palo Alto: Kodansha International, 1967.

Peter Swann, *Art of China, Korea, and Japan*. New York: Praeger. London: Thames and Hudson, 1963.

Tosaku Yoshioka and Sho Hiraoka, "Copper-Ruby Glaze, I and II," *Journal of the Japanese Ceramic Association*, vol. 35, 1927, p. 608, and vol. 36, 1928, p. 154; reported in "Abstracts," pp. 4 and 52, *Transactions of the British Ceramic Society*, vol. 28, 1928-29.

INDEX

ACG (ancient Chinese glazes), 29-32; example for glaze calculation. 117-122

Aging, glaze, 75, 103

Alkaline glazes, 16; and crazing, 44, 79; and turquoise, 79

Alpine, A.D., kiln company, 18

Alumina, 72, 79; content in water used in a glaze, 81

Andrews, A. I., 115

Applying, 17-18, 91; celadons, 31, 34, 35; combined glazes, 97-100; copper reds, 72; crystallized glazes, 75, 81; on-glaze decoration, 94, 98-99; turquoise glazes, 81-82; white slips, 113

Atomic weights, table of, 125

Attribution, 23-24, 38, 47-48

Baffle, glaze, 18, 91-92.

Ball Mill, 16; construction and use, 132-134

Batch weight, conversion from empirical formulas, 117-126

Bats, 17, 18; plaster, used for drying wood ashes, 16; wallboard, 17

"Blushes," 98-99

Bricks, insulating, 18, 19, 21

Bubbles, in glaze structure, 21, 36, 38, 39, 43, 69, 84, 105

Calcining clay-like materials, 85

Calcium, and turquoise glazes, 79

Carbon dioxide, 20; entrapped, 78, 112; in silicon carbide, 78

Cedar Heights clay, 112-113

Celadons, 23-24, 29-48, 93; Kinuta, 34, 36; Northern, 27, 41-43; Yüeh, 38, 47

Chang, elder, 43

Chien ware, 99. See also Temmoku

Chinese Art Treasures exhibition, 48

Ch'ing dynasty, 30, 40, 79. See also K'ang Hsi

Ching, Hsü, 47

Chuck, clay, 18

Chün, 15-21, 23, 24, 27, 39, 48, 69, 93, 108-109; and clay body, 21; and copper red decoration, 98; and synthetic wood ash, 130-131

Clay: bodies, 21, 24, 27; Cedar Heights, 112-113; Dalton #93, 112; earthenware, 83; fire, 112; secondary, 106, 107; stoneware, 111-113

Cobalt, used as a colorant, 79, 80, 86, 90

Combined glazes, 97-100

Cone pat, 19

Consistency, glaze, 17, 18, 42, 81

Contraction, 43

Cook, Ralph J., 116

Copper oxide, 70, 73, 76, 77

Copper reds, 48, 69-82; and Chün, 98; local reduction, 77-78; as on-glaze decoration, 98-99; oxblood, 69-73; peach bloom, 69, 71, 73-78; reduced, 69

Corn syrup, 73. See also Gum

Cox, Paul E., 44

Crab's claw, 44

"Cracking" the kiln, 21

Crackle glazes, 37, 43-47; causes of, 43, 44; Ko, 43-47; staining 45, 46-47

Crawling, 18, 31; and copper reds, 72, 75

Crazing, 35, 37, 43-44, 48, 79; encouraging, 44-47; and oxblood, 69; versus dunting, 66

Crystallization, 81, 84; in oxblood and peach bloom, 71, 72, 75; in temmoku, 88-89

Dalton #93 clay, 112
Dark brown temmoku, 86–87
Deep black temmoku, 83, 84–86
Drying: wood ash, 16; glaze, 18
Dunting, 21, 84, 103; versus crazing, 66

Earthenware, 83
Empirical formulas, calculating glazes from, 117–126
Emperor Ch'ien Lung, 47, 48
Epidote, 104, 123; preparing, 106
Eutectics, 27, 30
Expansion, 43
Experiments: with combined glazes, 97–100; with found materials, 103–108; with new glazes, 65, 67

Feldspar: and crazing, 44; Fukishima, 129; potash, 16, 35, 36; soda, 32, 35, 36
Figges, John, and Fujio Koyama, 99, 100
Fireholes, 18
Firing, 19–21, 66–67; neutral condition in, 67; oxblood and peach bloom, 75–76
Flambé, 69, 72
Flame-color check, 20
Flint, 44
Flue opening, 18, 20, 21
Fogg Art Museum, Harvard University, 98
Foot: cleaning, 18; and iron oxide wash, 90, 103; unglazed, 21, 91–92
Fukishima feldspar, 129

Garner, Sir Harry, 34, 47
Glaze calculation, 115–126
Gompertz, G. St. G. M., 38, 47
Granite powder, 31, 32, 35, 65, 123; calculating a glaze using, 120–122; percentage analysis, 32
Gray, Basil, 34
Gum, 17, 99; used for bonding resists, 98

Han dynasty, 29
Hare's fur, 83, 87, 99, 105; effects, 97
Hayashiga, Seizo, and Gakuji Hasebe, 99
Hematite. See Granite Powder
Hetherington, A.L., 33, 76, 78, 87, 98
High-lime celadon. See Lung-ch'üan
Hobson, Robert L., 47
Holleman, David, 83
Honey, W.B., 38
Hsüan-tê, 69

Imperial ware, 24
Interior glazing, 17
Iridescence, in oil spot glazes, 86

Iron, 16, 21, 25, 27, 125; and celadons, 32; glazes, 65–67; oxide, 30, 40, 76; silicate, 30, 41; and volcanic ash, 108; wash, 90, 103, 113
Ishii (Japanese glaze researcher), 30
Issu-wood ash, 127

Ju ware, 25, 38, 47–48

K'ang Hsi, 69, 74, 75
Kaolin, 29, 30, 79
Kiln(s): Chinese, 19; cracking, 21; electric, 78; for local reduction, 78; natural gas, 18, 20, 78; overfiring, 46; pyrometer, 19, 20; stacking, 18–19, 27; updraft, 18
"Kiln transmutation," 99, 100
Ko, 43–47
Korean ceramics, 38
Koryo, 38–41, 42, 47, 48
Koyama, Fujio, and John Figges, 99, 100
Kuan, 21, 24, 25, 27, 34–38, 48, 93; blue-green 36, Ko-type, 34, 37, 43–47
Kuan-Chün, 23–27; procedures, 25; stacking, 27

Laufer, Berthold, 29
Leach, Bernard, 107, 127
Lithium, 33, 41, 124; via spodumene, 41
Lizard skin. See Temmoku
Local reduction. See Reduction, local
Lung-ch'üan, 24, 29–34, 43, 47, 93; combined formulas, 33; high-lime, 29–30

Magnesium, 30, 124; and turquoise glazes, 79
Mellor, J.W., 76, 78
Microcrystalline glaze structure, 26
Milling: dry, 16, 17, 25; found materials, 106; over-, 103; wet, 17, 21, 25
Ming dynasty, 69
Mixing, 16–17
Molecular weight, 116–126; table, 123–124
Monoxide group. See RO group
"Moon glow," 35
Moore, B., 76, 78

Narcissus pot, 48
Neutral condition in firing, 67
Nichols, H.W., 29, 30, 115
Nomori (Japanese glaze researcher), 38
Northern celadon, 27, 41–43; with molded surfaces, 41

Oil spot, 25, 83, 86, 89
On-glaze decoration, 94, 98–99, 114
Ōnishi, Masatarō, 128, 129
Opalescence, 42, 73; in copper reds, 71, 72

Oxblood, 69–73; firing procedures, 75–76; and local reduction, 77; physical structure, 76–77

Oxidation, 20, 25; and clay color, 21; and copper reds, 75, 78; and oil spot, 86, 89; and on-glaze decoration, 94; after reduction, 75, 76; and temmoku, 90; and turquoise glazes, 82

Oxygen, aerial, 76–78

Parmelee, Cullen, 29, 115, 116

Partridge feather, 89–92

Patterson, J.B.E., 127

Peach bloom, 69, 71, 73–78; and crystallization, 75; firing procedures, 75–76; physical structure, 77

People's ware, 93

Percival David Collection, London, 47

Père d'Entrecolles, 19, 47

Phosphorus, 16, 21, 107

Placement, kiln. See Kiln, stacking

Plaster bats. See Bats

Potash feldspar, See Feldspar, potash

Potassium oxide, 79, 124

Potter's Book, A, 127

Reduction, 18–19, 20, 21, 24, 25; and celadons, 30, 32; clay color, 21; and copper red, 69, 75; and crazing, 44; and glaze combinations, 100; heavy, 19, 20, 30, 112; and iron glazes, 66–67; local, 77–78, 108; and oxblood, 75; with oxidation, 65–67; and temmoku, 89, 90

Resists: masking tape, 98; paper, 97, 98

Rinsing wood ash, 17

RO group, 116

Saggers, 19

Sanders, Herbert, 40, 45, 127–129

Sang-de-boeuf. See Oxblood

Screening wood ash, 16

Secondary clay. See Clay, secondary

Shino glaze, 40, 45

Silica, 16, 30, 44, 72

Silicon carbide, 77, 78, 108

Siltstone glaze, 44

Siphon, 17

Slate powder, red, 83, 84

Slip, white, 38, 113; under copper red, 72–73; under Kuan, 34–35; under turquoise glazes, 80; under Tz'u-chou, 93–96

Slumping, 112

Soaking, 86

Soda ash. See Sodium oxide

Sodium oxide, 16, 79, 80, 81, 124

Soluble substances, in wood ash, 16

Spodumene. See Lithium

Spraying: equipment, 17; glaze, 91, 97; side-by-side glaze combinations, 98; techniques, 17–18; white slip, 113

Stacking, 18–19, 27

Stains, 113; and crackle glazes, 46–47

Stoneware, 111–113

Storing wood ash, 16

Sung dynasty, 23, 29, 38, 41, 43, 69, 79, 83, 90, 93

Synthetic wood ash, 107, 127–131

Tea dust, 83, 87–89

Temmoku: dark brown, 86–87; deep black, 84–86; from found clay, 105; hare's fur, 83, 87, 89–92; lizard skin, 87; oil spot, 25, 83, 84–86; partridge feather, 89–92; streaked, 89–92, 106; tea dust, 83, 87–89; from traprock, 106

Tin oxide, 124; and oxblood, 70, 73, 76; and peach bloom, 73

Translucency, 15, 29, 34, 40, 86

Traprock, 106; obtaining, 107

Turquoise, 79–82, 93; and white slip, 80

Tz'u-chou, 93–96, 113

Underglaze decoration, black, 80, 94, 96, 114

Vivianite, 21

Volcanic ash, 108–109

Wall, E.F., 32

Water, added to glaze, 42, 71, 81; and cleaning ashes, 16

Wells-Lamson Quarry Company, 32

White Slip. See Slip, white

Wood ash: and celadon, 29, 32, 36, 42; and Chün, 15–16; "common," 128–129; drying, 16; hardwood, 25; issu, 127; mixed-wood, 35; nature of, 24; obtaining, 107; preparing, 15–17; rinsing, 17; screening, 16; softwood, 15, 35, 40, 65; synthetic, 16, 107, 127–131; and temmoku, 88; and Tz'u-chou, 94

Work-heat, 19, 44, 65

World of Japanese Ceramics, The, 127, 128

"Worm tracks," 25, 26

"Yao pien," 99

Yellow ochre, 21; and brushed-on-glaze effects, 94, 113

"Yohen," 99